# SOCIAL SKILLS

## FOR TEENS

*A Simple*
**7 Day**
*System for*
*Teenagers*

*to Break Out of Shyness, Build*
*a Bulletproof Self-Confidence,*
*and Eliminate Social Anxiety*
*to Excel in Social Interactions*

 **EMILY CARTER**

# TABLE OF CONTENTS

# YOUR FREE GIFT

Having the right mindset is the key when it comes to achieving success in any area of your life. As a way of saying thank you for your purchase, I want to offer you my book *Unleashing Your Potential: A Teenager's Guide to Developing a Growth Mindset and Opening Your Path to Success* for completely FREE of charge.

To get instant access, just scan the QR-code below or go to: https://lifeskillbooks.com/social-skills-free-bonus

Inside the book, you will discover...

✦ The difference between a fixed and growth mindset, how your mindset impacts your personal growth and success, and why a growth mindset is the one you should adopt.

✦ Practical strategies to cultivate a growth mindset, from daily habits to overcoming obstacles.

✦ How to utilize a growth mindset to supercharge your academic and career success.

✦ And much more!

But wait, there's more to come...

In addition to the *Unleashing Your Potential* eBook, I want to give you two additional special bonuses:

# BONUS 1

*The Essential Summer Job Handbook: The Teen's Guide to a Fun and Profitable Summer*

Inside this exciting guide, you will discover...

✦ The many benefits of having a summertime job, from earning extra cash to gaining valuable experience and skills that will set you up for success in the future.

✧ The different types of jobs available for teens at different ages, and how to market yourself effectively to potential employers.

✧ Practical tips for avoiding being taken advantage of, and advice on tax considerations that every working teen needs to know.

# BONUS 2

*Raising Teens With Confidence: 10 Exclusive Blog Posts on Parenting Teens*

I know this sounds boring if you're a teen, and that's completely fine. But for you parents out there, these unreleased blog posts offer a great opportunity to learn some new effective ways of parenting your teen.

Inside this compilation, you will discover…

✧ Invaluable insights and practical tips on how to navigate the challenges of parenting teenagers, from setting boundaries and dealing with mood swings to managing serious issues like drink and drug use.

✧ How to pick your battles wisely and let go of the small stuff, while still maintaining a strong connection with your teen and encouraging them to open up to you.

✧ Effective strategies for getting your teen to help out more at home, and how to strike the right balance between being a supportive parent and allowing your teen to develop their independence.

If you want to really make a change in your life for the better and get ahead of 95% of other teens, make sure to scan the QR-code below or head to the web address below to gain instant access to your bonuses.

https://lifeskillbooks.com/social-skills-free-bonus

# INTRODUCTION

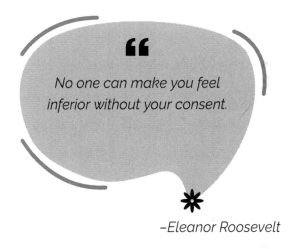

**"**

*No one can make you feel inferior without your consent.*

✳

*–Eleanor Roosevelt*

✦ ✦ ✦ ✦

While it's a good quote—a great one even—I have some notes. First of all, as much as we try to deny it, we are not in control of our thoughts and emotions. Sure, there are a lot of mental exercises and practices that can improve our self-awareness and emotional intelligence, which might lead us to better understand (and control) our *reactions* to the world around us—and to what goes on in our minds when life happens.

1

However, to say that we can choose not to be offended, hurt, or made to feel inferior to others' words and actions is implying we should deny or ignore our thoughts and emotions altogether. And honestly, I'm offended by that. We can learn how to respond to our emotions in a way that's healthy, but there's no magical switch you can flip to suddenly not care; this isn't *The Vampire Diaries*.

Now, you might be thinking, what do our emotions have to do with building confidence and self-esteem in social interactions? And the answer is: Probably more than you might realize. You see, your emotions shape your perspective on life, and perspective controls your thoughts, and your brain will believe everything it tells itself because it's biased.

Each and every one of us have what are called "automatic thoughts." These are thoughts that are influenced by things like past experiences, perspectives, and emotional triggers. If your automatic thoughts are negative by nature, they can wreak havoc on the way you see yourself, especially if you're still getting to know who you are and where you fit into the world as a teenager.

"I'm just introverted," your brain might say. And that might be true, but there's a difference between preferring to be alone and feeling like you're not socially capable of building meaningful relationships. Introverts are still confident in their ability to interact with the world; they just don't feel the need to.

If the only reason you don't like talking to other people is because it feels hard, you never seem to know what to say, you believe they don't like you based on zero evidence, you feel you're too awkward, you assume they're judging you, or you believe they're better than you, then you might not actually be an introvert after all.

Your inner monologue can make you believe things so strongly that you don't even question them. And it's only when you make a conscious effort to challenge your own beliefs, values, and perspectives that you start the process of rewiring your brain to be kind and more accepting of your flaws and perceived shortcomings. Becoming aware of your self-sabotaging thought processes and tendencies is the first step to a healthier self-image.

Building and practicing social skills in your teen years are important for a few reasons. Mainly because, as an adult, it's necessary to be willing and able to communicate effectively in unfamiliar circumstances. Whether it's for work, friendships, or romantic relationships, social skills are the foundation of any meaningful interaction. It helps avoid miscommunications, resolve conflict, build trust, set boundaries, and so much more.

If you think about it, the absolute best time to work on these skills—and practice using them—is during your teen years. Sure, you might make a fool of yourself once or twice, but everyone is so focused on themselves and their own presence in the world at this age that your mishaps go unnoticed most of the time. When you compare how many cringeworthy moments you've had to what you remember your peers having, it paints a clear picture.

The thing is, you don't remember their awkward moments because they've had less of them; you just don't think it's worse than yours. And that right there is a prime example of how powerful the brain can really be. It would be foolish to assume that they're watching and waiting for you to do or say something embarrassing as much as they're trying not to do or say something embarrassing themselves.

But let's say they do make a big deal of something you did or said. Oftentimes, when others are inflating your misgivings, it comes from a place of low self-esteem and a lack of confidence in themselves. It's a way to redirect attention away from themselves, so they can feel secure and lower their guard—even if just for a moment. It's never fun to be in a situation like that, but how you respond to it (regardless of how you feel) can make a world of difference to how others perceive you and your self-confidence.

The anxiety that comes with low self-esteem and social interaction is not going to go away on its own. Unfortunately, you're going to have to face your fears at some point or another, and it all starts with rebuilding the foundations of a positive self-image and finding your voice.

You might be thinking, "It's impossible to build confidence and overcome social anxiety in only seven days." And, of course, you'd be absolutely right. The idea— or my idea, at least—of the seven-day system is to build a habit. When you know exactly what to do every single day, and you have a clear strategy and plan in place, you're not left wondering what you should be doing.

Week after week, you follow the same steps of doing something small and seemingly insignificant every day until you've built up enough tolerance to face your fears (or hesitation) surrounding social interaction. Only once you're able to go through every exercise comfortably do you move on to more advanced or intimidating situations.

Throughout this book, we'll be doing just that. You'll learn effective and easy ways to work on personal growth, communication skills, and handling difficult or awkward situations using a seven-day system that will kickstart your journey to self-discovery and self-acceptance.

And remember, social skills—just like any other skill— require practice and perseverance (even when it's hard).

By taking one tiny step at a time, you'll build tolerance and maybe even realize that it's not half as bad or difficult as you may have thought.

## CHAPTER 1

# Day 1    SELF-AWARENESS

> **"**
>
> *We don't see things as they are,*
> *we see them as we are.*

–Anais Nin

✦✦✦✦

T he term "self-awareness" gets thrown around a lot, and I believe that a lot of people don't truly understand what it means. Everyone is technically aware of themselves, but an overused profound quote that gets posted alongside a selfie with a grayscale filter on it isn't exactly the epitome of self-awareness.

Don't get me wrong; I hold cheesy philosophical quotes very near and dear to my heart. A lot of them inspire creative thinking, ideas, introspection, and new perspectives. The way that everyone can look at the exact same piece of art, for example, and come up with their own unique interpretations of what's happening based on their own unique set of brainwaves, the emotions they think it's meant to conjure, and the general "vibe" or meaning they personally look for behind it will forever fascinate me.

## Levels of Self-Awareness

You are not born self-aware; it's something that develops over time—much like self-image. It's how you make sense of the things you do based on your opinions, emotions, values, and belief systems. There are five key elements (or levels) of self-awareness:

1. **Consciousness.** By the age of five, you'll have the basic understanding that you're a person with your own thoughts, emotions, and experiences. You can recognize your own reflection and identify yourself in a picture or video.

2. **Self-knowledge.** You know your current likes, dislikes, and preferences. It also includes your motivations, beliefs, and opinions.

3. **Emotional intelligence.** This is your ability to understand, manage, and express your emotions in a healthy way.

4. **Self-acceptance.** You're able to recognize your flaws and admit mistakes while still showing kindness and compassion for yourself.

5. **Self-reflection.** You reflect on your emotions and behaviors and whether or not they align with who you believe yourself to be. You use this feedback for self-improvement rather than self-hatred.

Furthermore, there are two distinct types of self-awareness: public and private. Public self-awareness is when there's a lot of attention on you from other people, like when you're delivering a speech or presentation—you have the spotlight. You're, therefore, hyper-aware that you're being watched and evaluated. This pressure usually causes us to behave in ways that are considered to be more socially acceptable. If you have social anxiety (or even something akin to "stage fright"), you're focused and concerned about what everyone might think of you–especially if you were to do something embarrassing or "wrong."

Private self-awareness is when you become aware of certain aspects, features, or traits about yourself privately. The way you feel or what you think when you look in the mirror, when you realize you forgot to study for a test and your stomach drops, when your crush walks into the classroom and your heart starts beating faster. These are all examples of private self-awareness. You can feel and recognize what's going on in your mind and body.

Being self-aware is a good thing; it allows us to put the things we do and feel into perspective. It allows us to become better people. However, it's possible to be overly self-aware— it's called being self-conscious.

Most—if not all—people experience bouts of self-consciousness every now and again. Honestly, it's impossible not to in the era of social media, unachievable societal expectations, and impossible beauty standards. But it's not normal to be experiencing excessive amounts of self-consciousness. If it's to the point where it's affecting your quality of life on a daily basis, it might be worth speaking to a mental health professional about.

## Limiting Beliefs and Self-Sabotage

As part of your self-discovery journey, you'll have to come face-to-face with the fact that it was you holding yourself back all this time. Now, you might not be ready to hear that just yet, and that's okay.

The brain is biased, and it will convince itself that something is true even when it isn't based on facts. These are called limiting beliefs, and while some limiting beliefs are necessary to keep us safe and to form a productive and healthy society (like believing you can't fly so you don't try to jump out the window of a ten-story building or believing that stealing is wrong so you stop yourself from hotwiring a car).

However, some of these limiting beliefs keep us from achieving goals, experiencing new and exciting things, or taking advantage of great opportunities. For example, you might think you don't have what it takes to be a doctor, so you settle for being a teacher. You might think you won't get into the college of your dreams, so you don't even apply.

You believe no one finds you interesting, so you sit alone at lunchtime.

There are unhelpful limiting beliefs, and they keep you stagnant, unable or unwilling to move forward, take on new opportunities, and grow as a person. Whether you have limiting beliefs about yourself, the world, or life in general, the first step is to identify them. And you do that by thinking about a goal you have had stored in the deepest pits of your medulla oblongata that never seemed to leave despite how many times you've shot it down.

This could be anything from learning a new skill to making new friends. Now, ask yourself why you aren't actively working on it. I can guarantee you there's a limiting belief somewhere surrounding it. For example, let's say you're into DIY and you've flipped furniture pieces for your own room. The idea of turning it into a side hustle has popped up in your head a couple of times, and even though it gets you excited every time, you haven't taken it further.

The limiting beliefs here can be that you don't think you have enough skill, knowledge, or creativity, or that no one would buy second-hand furniture from a teenager. See how none of these beliefs are rooted in reality? How none of them are based on evidence or facts?

If you're still having trouble identifying your limiting beliefs, here are a few alternative ways (besides thinking of a goal you're not working toward and why) that might bring more clarity:

✧ **Get rid of mind clutter.** Your mind, just like your desk or your bedroom floor, can get cluttered if you don't make an effort to get rid of all the unnecessary thoughts. Unnecessary thoughts are things that stick around in your mind and can be hard to get rid of: Fears and worries, wants and desires, the upcoming test you haven't studied for, your to-do list, negative experiences, lingering emotions, things you can't control, and so on. Either way, having too much going on upstairs makes it harder to think clearly or focus on anything. The easiest and most effective way to reduce and prevent mind clutter from accumulating to an overwhelming level is to write it out. The act of putting your thoughts onto paper (or even typing it out in your notes app) helps you let go of these unnecessary and negative thoughts. You could also try meditating, taking a nap (and making sure you're getting enough sleep in general), decluttering your physical environment (i.e., cleaning your room), spending some time in the sun, limiting external distractions and stimuli for a bit, or adding ten minutes of physical activity to your daily schedule. Keep what works; leave what doesn't.

✧ **Be curious.** Limiting beliefs are often associated with being closed-minded, and closed-mindedness is synonymous with having a fixed mindset (the idea that we can't change who we are or improve ourselves to any degree). You can start working on moving toward a growth mindset by adopting an "everything is figureoutable" mentality and being curious about yourself, your past experiences, and your current sense of reality (and whether it's possible that it might be warped). So be curious, doubt your mind's intentions for you, ask questions, and challenge yourself.

✧ **Work on self-improvement.** Self-improvement is kind of the entire goal of this book. And by admitting change is needed, being willing to change, and being open to the words written on these pages, you have already taken the first step! But self-improvement isn't a one-and-done type of deal; it's a life-long journey—one that is continuously changing who you are for the better. As part of the first step in self-improvement, you'll need to dig deep and identify your personal values. This is a list of what's most important to you in life. To identify your core values, start by answering the following questions:

- Think of a time (or times) when you felt most at peace, happy, or fulfilled. Who were you with, and what were you doing?

- Think of a time (or times) when you felt hurt, angry, or unhappy. What happened?

- What inspires you the most?

- What are you most proud of?

- If you could change anything about the world, what would it be?

Based on these answers, you should be able to see certain themes pop up. Maybe a majority of the moments when you were most happy were with family—you value family. Your worst moments were when someone betrayed or lied to you—you might value honesty, trust, and loyalty. If music inspires you, you could value creativity. And so on. By the end of this exercise, you should have a good idea of what your core values are. You can then do some soul-searching and define them better, add new ones, and remove ones you don't strongly identify with—until you're left with just a handful. This doesn't mean they can't change over time as you grow and gain new perspectives, but it's a pretty good starting point. You might also discover you have some unhelpful or negative core values, such as valuing money a bit too much, being dishonest at times, the need for attention or being liked all the time, being rude, superiority, entitlement, and so on. If you do find you have a couple of negative core values, these are the ones you focus on correcting while on your journey to self-improvement.

✧ **Counseling.** There comes a point where all the self-help books in the world won't help you break free from the shackles of your own mind. If you think you might already be too far down the rabbit hole, rest assured there's still hope. I can only give you so much advice and cheesy philosophical quotes from here. Sometimes you need someone right there with you on your self-discovery journey that can give you personalized support and course correct you when you veer too far from the path. Therapists and counselors can help, and there's nothing wrong with needing support until you can take the reins and continue on your journey alone.

## Self-Acceptance 101

Self-acceptance doesn't mean making excuses for your bad habits or bad behaviors; it simply means acknowledging them, being aware of them, and admitting you need to work on them without creating resentment toward yourself. It also means being proud of your accomplishments, your progress, your contributions, and your skills.

Someone who is self-aware is able to view themselves realistically. They know what their strengths are and don't feel insecure about their weaknesses. For example, they don't look at a video of Tony Hawk skateboarding online and think they're useless because they can't perform at that same level.

Someone who accepts themselves will see themselves as a whole person with flaws, quirks, emotions, traits, and past experiences instead of defining themselves based on a certain or singular incident, ability, characteristic, or weakness. They believe they are worthy of respect and love because their sense of value comes from within—they respect, value, and love themselves unconditionally.

The good news is, you can become this person too!

Once you've identified your core values, you can adjust your actions accordingly. This strengthens your sense of identity so you feel more grounded and able to challenge negative self-talk and distorted thoughts.

Practice self-compassion and standing up to yourself, for yourself. Negative self-talk and distorted thoughts are a result of those pesky cognitive biases we talked about earlier. The more you entertain negative self-talk and allow them to go unchallenged, the stronger they get. Then, just like Mario when he eats a mushroom, they grow into distorted thoughts. When this happens, the constant negative self-talk has done its job and the distorted thoughts and beliefs take on a life of their own.

Distorted thoughts and beliefs can make spotting negative self-talk more challenging, but with a bit of practice and conscious effort, you'll be able to deconstruct your entire self-image and build it back up stronger and more accurately.

## Self-Assessment

You can't accept yourself if you don't know who you are. Not only is knowing who you are necessary for self-acceptance and self-improvement, but it also plays a huge role when it comes to setting goals for yourself in every aspect of life. If something isn't important to you, if you're not good at it, or if it goes against who you are, you're not going to make progress in a way that's meaningful to *you*. And that defeats the whole purpose of life.

Let's start with something simple: What do you like to do? Keep it as broad and general or as detailed as you want. Look at your day-to-day life; what do you look forward to every day? Maybe you enjoy the bike ride home from school, the earthy smell when it just starts to rain, reading, listening to indie music, cosplaying, playing video games, rearranging your room, roller skating, watching movies, ASMR. Maybe you actually like pineapple on pizza!

Nothing is insignificant; even the small things—that many other people might also like to do—are what make up who you are.

Now ask yourself the opposite: What do you not like or not like doing? Start with the biggest, most obvious things like maybe school, homework, chores, and vegetables, if applicable. Once these are out of the way, go deeper. Maybe you don't like the color red, going into direct sun, taking a bath (because in your mind it's like making human soup), exercising, wearing jeans, the taste of artificial grape flavor, and so on.

The next question you're going to ask yourself is: What are you good at? You may find that the things you're good at are closely related or overlap with the things you enjoy doing. You like playing chess because you rarely lose. You like baking because it always turns out great. Maybe you actually enjoy school because you love learning new things, and you get good grades. You get the point. Evaluate the things you're good at to find the soft life skills that often lurk beneath the surface: Creativity, patience, kindness, curiosity, determination, and many more.

You probably saw this coming, but the next question is obviously: What are you bad at? The answers to these might also be in relation to the things you don't like doing, or it might be because you simply have no interest in them. For example, you might tell yourself that you're bad at socializing because you have no interest in it when in reality, you're just bad at socializing. So be honest with yourself here. Because being bad at something can be fixed, having no interest in it is a different story.

You can write down your answers to all of these questions separately and keep it as a reminder that you are a whole person—which includes the good and the bad. Try to approach your answers from an analytical standpoint (no judgment, just curiosity). Come back to it every now and then to add to the lists, take things away that no longer apply, or just read through it for fun.

If it helps, you can also find self-assessment tests online, which include personality tests. Though, I would advise using personality tests as rough or inspirational guidelines only since they tend to be anecdotal (not to mention your own bias can influence the results greatly). Don't take them at face value, is all I'm trying to say.

Once you know your true strengths, weaknesses, interests, values, and beliefs, you have a pretty good idea of who you are—in theory. Now, you might not be ecstatic about what you discovered about yourself in the process. No one is 100% happy with who they are. But again, self-acceptance isn't about whether you like who you are; it's about acknowledgment.

"Am I flawed?" Yes. "Do I still deserve love, compassion, empathy, and respect?" Yes, just like everyone else.

Self-acceptance means to treat yourself the way you would a close friend or loved one. You'd never tell someone you love that they're not good enough, not pretty enough, not talented enough, or not smart enough. And if you would say something like this to someone you care about, you need to acknowledge that your values and behavior toward others are bad and toxic, and take accountability for it.

But either way, the call is coming from inside the house. Whether you treat yourself badly or treat others badly, it's your responsibility to see the light, see that it doesn't serve you, and willingly choose to do the work in order to change for the better.

## Self-Actualization

There's a lot of debate around what the term "self-actualization" really means. Some say it's the act of becoming who you were meant to be as a person; others say it's about reaching your fullest potential. But for the sake of our purposes, I'm going to define it as becoming the best possible version of yourself.

However, while self-actualization can be interpreted in a lot of different ways, none of the definitions involve being perfect. Unrealistic expectations, perfectionism, or anxiety about making the "right" choice can actually hinder your progress when trying to live authentically.

Becoming the best version of yourself is about living your life in a way that takes full advantage of your strengths while also taking your limits (or weaknesses) into consideration.

People who are actively being who they were meant to be (or self-actualized individuals) don't let what other people think of them get in the way of their reality and truth; they don't depend on external approval or validation. They let their creativity, intuition, and spontaneity guide them, they don't pretend to know things to impress others, and they are comfortable with uncertainty and constructive criticism. They don't take themselves too seriously, and they can admit when they've made a mistake and take responsibility for their actions and behaviors. They dedicate themselves to doing things that bring purpose, happiness, and fulfillment to their own lives while not harming others in the process. They consider the bigger picture while also being able to appreciate the smaller things in life.

Self-actualization goes hand-in-hand with self-awareness and self-improvement. In fact, working toward being more self-aware and wanting to improve yourself will most likely put you on the path to self-actualization, whether you like it or not. There's no endgame here; all of it is a lifelong journey without a destination.

## Daily Task

Becoming self-aware takes practice and time. It's not going to happen after just one self-assessment session. It's not a possession; it's a skill. It's the ability to analyze your thoughts, habits, actions, and emotions—without judgment—and determine whether they are true to who you really are or who you want to become. And then gradually and consciously working toward positive change until the changes become subconscious or automatic.

This is why your first daily practice or task will be to start journaling. Regardless of whether you think it's silly, intimidating, or embarrassing—just try it. Challenge yourself: Journal every day for a week, and then stop for a week. Pay close attention to how you felt during the week you were journaling versus the week when you weren't.

Document the results by giving your mental clarity or general state of mind a rating (out of 5 stars, or 0–10, for example) every day during the two weeks of the challenge so you can compare your findings accurately.

If there's a visible improvement in your ratings during the week you were journaling and then a steady decline during the week you weren't journaling, you should continue the habit (and you owe me $5). If there's no improvement, or your rating gets worse when journaling, then journaling probably isn't for you, and you should maybe look into different ways to improve self-awareness—there are plenty to choose from, so don't panic.

And to prevent you from backing out because you don't know where to start or what to write about, I'm going to walk you through a few ideas and prompts to inspire your one-week daily writing challenge:

- **Day 1: What are three things that challenged me today, and how did I handle it?**

  This could include physical, mental, or emotional challenges of any degree of difficulty or significance. You couldn't find your socks this morning, you missed the bus, you messed up your verbal assignment, your dad was in a bad mood when he got home, the batteries in your controller dead, you have to work in a group for a project with someone you don't like, PE class, the girl you liked rolled her eyes at you. Anything goes!

  Then write down how you handled it, what you did before, during, and after, how it made you feel, and any further information that's relevant (or not relevant, it's *your* journal). Now, write how you think you should've handled it based on your ideal values and beliefs—only if how you handled it in reality doesn't align with who you want to be. And what you can do to realize these changes if you were to ever be in that situation again.

  You can also write about life challenges you face in general, not just for the day.

O **Day 2: What are my three most recent limiting beliefs, and why are they not true?**

It might help to think about recent situations where you found yourself holding back or avoided doing something. For example, you avoided showing your art to someone, you held back when doing a presentation, or you avoided having a discussion with your parents about something that's bothering you.

Now dig deeper. Try to remember the thought that came to mind or the reasoning behind why you didn't do something. The personal reasons you have for not doing something are, more often than not, due to a limiting belief. Sure, there are instances when holding yourself back from doing something is valid, for instance, when it involves hurting other people unnecessarily in any way.

But when it involves you doubting your experience, abilities, or value, it's a limiting belief that doesn't serve you. Once you have your three recent limiting beliefs, challenge them. It might help to not think about them as your own limiting belief but rather something someone you care about said to you about themselves. What reasons or assurances would you give them in order to convince them it's not true?

O **Day 3: What is something nobody knows about me?**

Again, it could be something small and superficial or deep and profound. It could be the first thing that comes to mind, maybe you already know the answer, or maybe you need to sit on it for a couple of minutes.

It could be anything that you haven't told anyone yet for whatever reason: a skill you taught yourself, a unique experience, a quirk or trait, a preference, a hobby, a hidden talent, or liking something controversial (like butter pecan-flavored ice cream). It could be as many things as you can think of or only one example. Take a second to let whatever it is resonate. You can expand on what you wrote down—the why's, what's, when's, and where's—or not.

The goal of this prompt isn't to justify, debunk, or prove anything but rather to appreciate yourself and acknowledge that you are a whole person regardless of what other people might think or say about you.

## O   Day 4: What things have I avoided doing because of fear?

It might help, once again, to think of a recent example since you might not remember specifics or details about something that happened years ago—but feel free to still write about a distant past experience.

This prompt in itself might help you uncover deeper or stronger self-limiting beliefs. Don't be scared to dive into it and give all your thoughts, emotions, and theories on the fear itself, what caused it, how it has impacted you now, and how it can potentially hinder your growth in the future.

## O Day 5: What do I need to let go of?

Let me be clear: Letting go of something and forgiveness is not the same thing. You can let go of something and move on while still holding someone accountable for their hurtful actions against you. Letting go of negative, debilitating thoughts, emotions, and experiences is about and for *you*. Forgiveness is for those who deserve it, but it's not necessary for healing.

With that in mind, think of a negative feeling or thought you've been holding onto for a long time. Write as much detail as you can remember about the incident. Don't hold back; let your emotions take over and spill out over the pages. Write until there's nothing more to write about, until every last drop of resentment, frustration, regret, or devastation has been captured in ink.

Feel the weight of having to hold on to this burden for so long slip off your shoulders, feel the negative emotions seeping out of your pores and vaporizing, feel the hold it has had on your heart loosening. Take the deepest breath you've taken the entire day, breathe as if it's the first time your lungs are filling with oxygen, and let go—whatever that means to you.

## O Day 6: What would my ideal life look like?

What would your ideal life look like right now with regard to yourself, your habits, your accomplishments, and your skills? Yes, it would be nice to live in a mansion, be driven (or drive) to school in the newest Mercedes, and have more money than you know what to do with. But that's not what I'm referring to with this question.

The more specific you are, the better. For example: "I would exercise and make my bed every day, I wouldn't freeze or stumble over my words when having a conversation, I wouldn't care what other people say or think about me, I wouldn't doubt my place in the world, I would get into that program," and so on.

This prompt is about self-discovery. But instead of saying everything you think you aren't or can't do and getting down about it, you're reframing it a bit. It might reveal things about you that you might've not considered, and it might make you aware of things you didn't know you wanted to do or become. And at the very least, it gives you an idea of future goals relating to self-improvement that you can start working on.

O **Day 7: If I had to choose a mantra or quote to live by, what would it be and why?**

Feel free to search for inspirational or meaningful quotes from philosophers, inventors, or whoever else tickles your fancy for ideas. Choose one that has a lot of meaning to you and explore why.

For example, my favorite quote that I live by is from Joshua J Marine: "Challenges are what make life interesting and overcoming them is what makes life meaningful" (2022).

The way I interpret this quote—and the reason why it's so meaningful to me—is that there will always be challenges in life, some bigger than others. Some mildly derail your plans or ruin your mood for the day, and others bring your entire world to the brink of collapse. There are a lot of things in life you can't change, but you can change your perspective. You can choose to overcome and learn from it. You can look back one day and see that everything turned out okay in the end anyway. You can admit that while it sucked at the time, it put into motion a butterfly effect that has gotten you to where you are today; it opened new doors and shut ones that you were too afraid to shut yourself.

The fact that I'm still here means that, so far, I have a 100% success rate at overcoming the biggest obstacles and challenges that I have faced. And that counts for something!

The seven prompts I provided above are for if you are the type of person who needs a guideline to follow or you don't know where to start. You can absolutely rearrange the order, make adjustments, or discard all of it and just write whatever comes up when the pen hits the paper—or your thumbs hit the screen. You can look up different prompts or ideas on what to write about, and you can create your own. There are no rules!

One suggestion I do have is that you stop here, do the first journaling prompt, and only continue on to the next chapter tomorrow. But keep journaling every day as you proceed with the daily tasks of the upcoming chapters. Doing this will prevent information overload.

## CHAPTER 2

# Day 2 — SELF-CONFIDENCE

*You're never as good as everyone tells you when you win, and you're never as bad as they say when you lose.*

–Lou Holtz

✦ ✦ ✦ ✦

As with many things in life, everyone has their own thoughts, feelings, and ideologies on what self-confidence actually means and what it looks like. Some people think it's good to be confident since it's connected to self-esteem, success, and good mental health; others think it's bad because they confuse it with vanity or narcissism.

According to the Merriam-Webster dictionary, the word "self-confidence" is defined as "Confidence in oneself and in one's power and abilities." Thanks, that's… revolutionary information.

Let's clear things up. Self-confidence means believing you have inherent value regardless of your mistakes; feeling worthy despite your flaws; respecting and loving yourself; having the courage to stand up to others and defend yourself; living in a way that feels true to who you are; and loving yourself as a whole.

As you can see, it can mean a lot of things—and all of them are accurate descriptions. But what being self-confident *doesn't* mean is that you're perfect or you need to be perfect; that you're better than others; that you should have and achieve high standards, goals, and expectations; that you won't have problems or struggles in life; that you can't be humble; or that you should be selfish.

## Developing A Growth Mindset

"You can't teach an old dog new tricks." A common saying implies that once a dog has reached a certain age, they are set in their ways and can't improve their behavior, skills, or abilities. Except, it's not true. One study that was published in 2016 shows that while older dogs might take longer to learn new tricks, it's still possible to teach them (Wallis et al., 2016). And this is only one of many.

But this phrase is also used amongst people, usually the older generations. In my opinion, using this term is a way to justify being stuck or stagnant. It's a way to get out of having to put in the work or effort to improve yourself. It's a way to absolve yourself of any responsibility regarding a need for change. It's lazy and outdated.

But this kind of mindset can happen to anyone at any age. It's called a fixed mindset and it will hold you back for your entire life. You have a fixed mindset if you believe that people are born with talent instead of having worked hard for years to develop it. You have a fixed mindset if you think there's a cap on what you're destined to become. You have a fixed mindset if you believe that not being good at or not knowing something is a permanent state of being.

People with a fixed mindset will avoid challenges because it could lead to failure, and since they believe that their attributes and skills can't be improved upon, failing at something means they are automatically a failure. It becomes so much more intense. They will also avoid or ignore constructive feedback from others (because they view it as a personal attack), feel threatened by others who achieve success, hide their flaws or mistakes, and give up easily.

When you believe that trying is futile, you become hopeless, and this only feeds into the narrative of someone with a fixed mindset. "I can't be better or do better, so why even try?" This black-and-white perspective of "you either *are* something or you're not" has a snowball effect on your self-confidence, self-esteem, self-image, and self-talk.

Getting out of a fixed mindset can be tricky because in order to do so, you first have to believe that change or improvement is possible—which literally goes against everything that someone with a fixed mindset believes. However, this is an instant where, once you've taken the first step, the most difficult part is already over.

## *What It Is*

Now that you know what a fixed mindset is—and whether or not you have one—let's talk about the alternative. A growth mindset is basically the complete opposite of a fixed mindset. Even if you don't have a fixed mindset (or you're not really sure and haven't given it much thought), you can still benefit from strengthening and developing a growth mindset.

So, what even is a "growth mindset?"

Well, a growth mindset means you view setbacks and failures as valuable—a necessary part of the learning process. Someone with a growth mindset recognizes that learning and the ability to learn has no expiration date. They are open to constructive criticism because it might bring forth ideas and perspectives that they might not have considered. They get inspired by the success of others and see challenges as opportunities to grow, learn, and improve.

Having a growth mindset has a huge positive impact on your motivation and academic performance and achievements. And that's a fact! (Yeager et al., 2019).

Here's another fact: You can change your mind. Even if you're stuck in the negative feedback loop and thinking patterns of a fixed mindset, you can rewire your brain to be more open to growth and learning.

### How To Change Your Mind

Don't get me wrong, changing your entire outlook on life will take time and practice, as most things do. But in my humble opinion, it's worth doing. What you need to understand is that if you believe anything, your brain will interpret and warp any information to prove itself to be right. There's that internal bias again.

And while there are certain things that will help you overcome a fixed mindset (like challenging your limiting beliefs and thoughts), I want to be even more specific about how you can go about changing your perspective—and, as a result, your mind.

⬥ **Know that, scientifically speaking, it's possible.** Your brain might not believe you if you simply tell it that developing, learning, and growing is possible. Luckily, there are studies that prove—without a doubt—that it is possible to change your mindset from negative (fixed) to positive (growth).

Neuroplasticity refers to the brain's ability to change, modify itself, and adapt its physical structure, as well as how it functions throughout your lifespan in response to various internal, external, and environmental factors (Voss et al., 2017). What this means is that your experiences and environment during childhood plays a huge role in how your brain's neural pathways form. These neural pathways are how your brain makes sense of the world around you and your pathways are different and unique to everyone else's—but they can also be changed or "rewired."

We see this with people who have lost one or more of their senses all the time. In someone who has undergone sensory loss, their remaining senses compensate for it. This is a prime example of neuroplasticity in the works. In order for their other senses to strengthen, their brain structure physically changes (Merabet & Pascual-Leone, 2009).

It's also proven that your thoughts have an effect on your emotions, and the stronger the emotional reaction to a thought, the more your brain believes it to be true. And since beliefs have the ability to change your brain structure (your neural pathways), it stands to reason that the only thing you need to do is change your beliefs. Sounds simple enough, right? However, it's exactly the "changing" part that many people struggle with. But again, just because it's going to take time and effort doesn't mean it won't happen or it's not worth it. So, in essence, the first and most important step in this journey is to convince yourself (through research and facts) that it is possible to change your mind.

✧ **Reward your efforts, not your results.** Remember, growing is a journey without a destination, which means that, oftentimes, you never get to see the end result. Stepping away from only feeling good about what you manage to accomplish and giving yourself a pat on the back for simply trying and making progress can be extremely validating and motivating.

For example, reward yourself when you manage to spot a limiting belief or negative thought, not just when you manage to successfully challenge or reframe it; reward yourself for recognizing that your body language might be telling people you're unapproachable, not just after you've fixed it.

Rewarding yourself could come in the form of anything you enjoy doing or what makes you feel good such as spending time in the sun, playing with a pet, having a movie night, taking a bubble bath, spending time on your favorite hobby, fixing yourself your favorite snack, and so on.

✧ **Relabel, reattribute, refocus, revalue.** Relabel negative thoughts as soon as you recognize them. If you did poorly on a test, for example, and your first thought is, *I'm so stupid*, pause and relabel it as anything other than true. Because it isn't. You can call it a brain glitch, a false message, an impulsive thought, a mental invasion, or anything else that questions the validity of the thought.

Reattribute the reason for having the thought in the first place to something that's out of your control. Because it is. Remind yourself that your mind is still stuck in a negative feedback loop based on old beliefs, experiences, and emotions. And that it's going to take a while to reprogram and get used to the new features and commands.

Refocus your attention to actively and consciously change your recurring negative thought patterns. This is when you replace the negative thought with one that's more realistic and accurate based on the evidence you have. Think of it as a manual override—since the automatic system is not doing what you need it to do. Using the example of automatically thinking you're stupid when you get a bad grade, you can counter it by following it up with, "Now hold on a second, since when does failing one singular test mean that a person is stupid in general? That doesn't seem like a fair analysis of overall intelligence." Go over the evidence and reality of the situation; maybe the truth is that you failed because you simply didn't study, studied the wrong material, or misunderstood a lot of the questions on the test. But again, none of the reasons for failing a test means you're not capable of passing the class in the end.

If you consistently follow the first three steps when negative thought patterns emerge, eventually, your brain will revalue them as mere distractions and untruths. Your mind catches up and drifts away from negative automatic responses because they don't hold as much weight anymore. Through practice and persistence, your relabeling, reattributing, and refocusing of negative thoughts will become easier and more automatic. You will have trained your brain to react with more positive and reality-based thoughts, which will also change your limiting beliefs.

✧ **Pay attention to what you're being exposed to.** This is especially true in the era of social media. The algorithms dictate what's on your feeds and "for you" pages. But the thing is, negativity is more popular than positivity—because it generates a stronger emotional reaction. You're more likely to react to, comment on, and stay tuned (or read) to the end of a post that talks about all the bad stuff that makes us lose faith in humanity.

But when you do this, you'll only be fed more of the same stories! I'm not going to go into how social media is all marketing and engagement, but just know that your mind will grow off of whatever you feed it. So be wise about the content that you consume.

But this also counts in real life. You can't control what other people do, say, or think, but you can remove yourself from certain situations or take steps to protect yourself and your mental health.

✧ **Tap into the power of "yet."** The word "yet" is a great subtle reminder that improvement and growth are possible. "I'm not able to identify and challenge all my limiting beliefs and thoughts—yet." "I'm not as confident in myself—yet." "My skill isn't on the level that I want it to be—yet," "I'm not very good at social interactions and situations—yet." It changes the narrative from hopeless to hopeful. It opens up a small window of possibility, and that's all you need to cram a crowbar in there and break it right open.

✧ **Build mental resilience.** Mental resilience refers to one's ability to adapt or recover from things like stress, emotional dysregulation, or other mentally exhausting challenges. And one thing you'll need on your journey to self-improvement through self-awareness is mental "toughness."

Mental resilience doesn't mean you should suppress or ignore your emotions or that you shouldn't have emotional reactions at all. It simply allows you to be courageous despite your doubts and fears, to stay in control of your thoughts and actions despite involuntary emotional responses, and to get where you want to be in life regardless of your past or current hardships.

How do you build mental resilience? By living life. By practicing and giving it time. By taking care of yourself, finding a purpose, establishing realistic goals and working toward achieving them, being mindful of how you talk to yourself, keeping things in perspective, and building meaningful connections. By accepting the things you can't change and finding a way to push through them anyway, you're proving to yourself (and strengthening the idea) that you're capable enough.

Believing in yourself—as corny as it might sound—really has a big role to play in self-confidence. In order to raise your confidence, you have to change the way you think of yourself and your true abilities. You do this by getting used to correcting your knee-jerk assumptions and automatic thoughts and slowly turning them around until they cave in on themselves.

## Building Self-Confidence

There's a reason why the majority of this chapter is filled with developing a growth mindset and setting goals. It's because believing that you are capable of improvement and achieving the goals you have been wanting to achieve (but might not have thought were possible) improves your self-esteem, and healthy self-esteem warrants self-confidence.

Self-esteem and self-confidence are a packaged deal; you can't authentically have one without the other—but they're separate concepts. Self-esteem is how you treat and value yourself in private and isn't always obvious from an outsider's perspective. Self-confidence is how you present yourself to the outside world and other people (and is typically based on self-esteem).

However, people with low self-esteem might present themselves as having a lot of self-confidence in order to make up for the former. In essence, "fake it 'till you make it." And while that sentiment might be helpful in many different, unrelated aspects of life, pretending to be confident in yourself only leads to a deeper identity crisis because you're living in two different realities where what you think and what you do doesn't line up—which may cause imposter syndrome (feeling like you're a fraud or you don't belong). It could also fuel anxiety and create mental exhaustion from always having to put on an act or a show—leading to eventual and complete social withdrawal and isolation.

Here's a fun fact: Opinions are not facts at all—not even when they're your own.

Your self-image is influenced by things such as your appearance, personality, the opinions of others, or past experiences. In a nutshell, your self-image is your opinion of yourself. It affects your behavior and how you interact with the world and other people. And most importantly, it affects your happiness, relationships, and overall well-being.

A negative self-image will impact the quality of your relationships. Whether that's because you doubt their intentions, aren't communicating your needs effectively, take constructive criticism personally, or feel like you can't be yourself around them, it all comes down to what goes on in your own head.

Expanding on that, people with low self-esteem might tolerate unhealthy or even abusive relationships because they will do mental gymnastics to excuse or defend the other person's behavior. They might even go as far as blaming it on themselves.

The inability to fully trust someone and open up to them will make it hard to connect on a deeper level, which will eventually lead them to believe that you're the one who's unwilling to build a relationship. As a result, they will withdraw, leaving you feeling confused and hurt once again, watering that now flourishing tree of doubt even more.

It's a vicious cycle, one that keeps you from living up to your potential, having people around you who care for you, and enjoying all the wonderful experiences that life has to offer.

Since self-esteem is the building block upon which self-confidence is built, it's easier to start there. So what can you do to work on improving your self-esteem?

First of all, stop comparing yourself to others. And yes, it's one of those things that's easier said than done. When the negative thoughts and emotional reactions start to creep in when looking at other people's lives, achievements, or success, do that thing where you challenge it. "I started my YouTube channel at the same time as [insert classmate's name here]. How come they have way more subscribers than me? That must mean I'm [insert limiting belief or cognitive distortion here]."

Now you follow up with the facts, but be careful not to assume things that you can't possibly know or verify. Sure, you may have started your respective channels at around the same time, but your niches and content are different; they post much more frequently than you and on a consistent schedule; they have better equipment and software, so their sound, lighting, and editing results in an overall better viewing experience. Maybe I could actually talk to them and find out what they're doing differently to me in terms of tags, titles, and all the other technical stuff.

See how the narrative changes? How it doesn't have to be so self-sabotaging and self-imposed?

It's normal to want to be extraordinary, and seeing others in a position that we want to be in right now can be demotivating. It rips our time and attention away from ourselves and our own goals and leaves us feeling defeated. Instead, compare yourself *with* yourself. But not in a mean, resentful type of way. Think of what you do differently today than you did yesterday. Did it improve your life? If not, think of what you can do today that your future self will thank you for.

Be your own hype man or woman. You can't always count on validation or acknowledgment from others, so tell yourself what you want to hear, be on your own side, comfort yourself, and reassure yourself—even if you don't believe it yet. Some additional small things you can do that will accumulate interest over time and build up your self-esteem—and inadvertently, your self-confidence—are:

✦ Make a list of things you're good at (big and small) and be proud of yourself for it.

✦ Stop focusing your attention on people who make you feel bad about yourself and gravitate toward people who are actually nice to you.

✦ Stop trying to convince people that you are cool, smart, chill, or whatever you think they want you to be or don't want you to be.

✦ Stop trying to please everyone with your words or actions; say "no" more often.

✧ Challenge yourself to step out of your comfort zone every day with small things and build up to bigger things.

✧ Stand up for yourself.

## Daily Task

Positive self-talk is advised to patients by licensed therapists as a way to combat negative or distorted thoughts, limiting beliefs, anxiety, stress, and even depression. It's a form of dialectical behavioral therapy (DBT) and it can have a huge impact on your overall mental and physical well-being and performance.

There are many ways to implement positive self-talk into your daily life, and the more you practice it, the easier and more natural it becomes. Negative thinking usually comes in four forms and can even overlap each other or occur simultaneously. The four forms of negative self-talk are:

✧ **Personalizing:** Blaming yourself for everything.

Example thought: *It would be so disappointing and inconsiderate of me if I change my mind.*

Corrected thought: *I have the right and power to change my mind, even if others might not understand.*

✧ **Magnifying:** Focusing so much on the negative—or even blowing them out of proportion—that you ignore any and all the positive aspects.

Example thought: *I completely embarrassed myself by doing that; I failed.*

Corrected thought: *It was hard to put myself out there like that, and I'm proud of myself for even trying, even if it didn't turn out the way I expected it to.*

✧ **Catastrophizing:** Always expecting the worst despite logic or reason.

Example thought: *There's no way I'm going to be able to accomplish that, so why even try?*

Corrected thought: *I will try my best; this is a great opportunity to learn something new.*

✧ **Polarizing:** You categorize everything as either all good or all bad with no middle ground.

Example thought: *I didn't clean my room; I am the laziest person in the world.*

Corrected thought: *I needed that hour of rest today; I'll get to it tomorrow.*

Something you can do every day that ties in with positive self-talk is words of affirmation. I've mentioned this earlier on, but positive affirmations are a set of affirming statements that you tell yourself every day. They could be the same or different every time, and it can form part of your self-care routine.

With that being said, taking care of yourself is very important for your self-esteem and will contribute to building unshakable self-confidence. In order to feel good about yourself, you need to take care of yourself. It reinforces the idea or belief that you are important—which you are—and that your well-being is important to you—as it should be.

And that is why today's task will be to say some positive things *about* yourself *to* yourself. It's going to feel awkward, but push through the cringe and try to really take them in. You can craft your own positive affirmations or choose the ones you like the most from the following list:

- ✧ I'm strong enough and capable of reaching my goals.
- ✧ I will grow and learn from my mistakes.
- ✧ I don't need to be perfect.
- ✧ I am worthy.
- ✧ I am enough.
- ✧ There is no shame in being wrong or making mistakes.
- ✧ I'm patiently changing into the person I want to become.
- ✧ Getting to know myself is exciting.
- ✧ What others think of me is not my responsibility.
- ✧ I get to decide what's best for me.
- ✧ It's okay that I don't have all the answers.
- ✧ I'm proud of myself.
- ✧ I give myself permission to be myself.
- ✧ I am allowed to feel my emotions.

✧  I am open to opportunities and challenges.

Please don't dismiss the power of positive affirmations until you've tried it. You can combine it with the journaling challenge or do it on its own. Choose different ones every day or recite the same ones. There's no wrong way to approach it; whatever works for you. But don't resist doing it because you're afraid of how it *might* make you look or feel—for starters, no one has to know that you're doing it; it's for you, not them. But also, stop assuming things and just give it a go for a couple of days. See how you feel then. Keep doing the things that help you, leave the things that don't—but at least do them first.

Remember, the journey isn't linear; you don't know what the future holds. It's okay to reassess your goals or methods for achieving them if things aren't working out or if you come to find that you want something completely different. You have the right to change your mind.

CHAPTER 3

## Day 3 · SOCIAL SKILLS

> **"**
>
> *Be courteous to all, but intimate with few, and let those few be well tried before you give them your confidence.*

*–George Washington*

✦ ✦ ✦ ✦

You might find you know most (or all) of the "rules" regarding socializing already based on common sense and experience alone, but it can't hurt to go over the principles and theoretical aspects of how to build rapport with others.

However, the last thing I want is for you to find yourself in a situation that's upsetting or severely uncomfortable before you're ready, which is why this chapter is going to go over the basics of socializing, social skills, and social cues. The goal of this chapter is to arm yourself with knowledge, that's all.

Knowing what to say, when to say it, and how to say something; knowing whether a conversation or interaction is going good or bad; and reading non-verbal cues and body language are all important factors to consider. But before you get overwhelmed, our subconsciousness picks up on most of this stuff already. The issue is that your subconscious mind might not always interpret things correctly. By being aware of social cues and how to respond to or interpret them, you ditch the guessing game altogether.

And by improving your social skills, you'll not only experience less social anxiety and be able to build stronger, more meaningful relationships, but it also raises your self-esteem and self-confidence as well as improves overall mental and physical well-being.

## The Basics

I find it ironic that social skills are so important, and yet we don't know exactly what they consist of. It's not like we're born grasping a pamphlet explaining this stuff, and it's also not something that's actively taught to us. I mean, the info is there; it's just not really presented to us in the same way as math or biology is. Okay, sure, the mitochondria are the powerhouse of the cell, but how much eye contact do I give before it's considered creepy?

Social skills and etiquette are necessary and important, especially once you enter the realm of young adulthood and beyond (which will come a lot sooner than you realize). One minute you're calling your mom "bro," and the next, you're getting excited in the home appliances aisle for 45 minutes.

My point is that humans are social creatures, and a lack of social skills can hold you back both from a personal and professional standpoint. Poor social skills might, for instance, ruin platonic and romantic relationships and be the cause for you not landing your dream job.

Social skills are how we express our feelings, communicate our thoughts, and relate to those around us. But being aware of how we do this is also important. It's not the easiest concept to wrap your head around. It's a lot to be aware of and pay attention to, and it's not like you've had much experience or time to polish these skills. So try not to feel bad about not having mastered the art of social interaction yet.

Before I go into detail on what individual skills make up "social skills," there are a few things I think are worth keeping in mind. First is that you don't need to get everything *just right* in order to build good and lasting relationships. You don't have to focus intently on just one factor or skill; they all work in unison. And you will mess up from time to time—even the most charismatic people can sometimes come across as rude or uninterested.

There are two main forms of communication, namely verbal and non-verbal. Verbal communication happens when you verbalize your thoughts, feelings, opinions, and ideas, either through talking or writing them down. Non-verbal communication happens through things like eye contact, gestures, facial expressions (including micro-expressions), and body language. Let's break that down.

## Verbal Communication

Many argue that your tone and volume of voice don't (or shouldn't) fall under verbal communication. For one, you can't really discern tone or volume through written text—unless they're typing in all caps, then it's safe to assume they are, in fact, shouting. Nonetheless, I do feel like the way you say something does affect how it's received.

A simple example of this is when you look at what happens to the underlying implication of the sentence when you place emphasis on certain words:

"**I** didn't say you should do it." Someone else said it.

"I **didn't** say you should do it." I explicitly told you not to do it.

"I didn't say **you** should do it." I said someone else should.

It's the exact same sentence, but it means something different depending on where you place the stress. Here are the most important individual elements that form part of effective (or ineffective) verbal communication:

✧ **Form of language.** Knowing when and how to use either informal or formal language. This doesn't necessarily mean having a large vocabulary with big fancy words. A simple example of this is not cursing or swearing when talking to an elderly lady or your principal.

- ✧ **Clarity.** Pronouncing words correctly and articulating sentences so you're coherent and easy to understand. Stating your thoughts or ideas with confidence.

- ✧ **Tone.** Where you place emphasis changes the meaning or intention behind a sentence. This influences how your words are received by others.

- ✧ **Pitch.** Raising or lowering the pitch in your voice for effect. An example of this is when you're being sarcastic or trying to imitate someone else.

- ✧ **Pace.** Talking slowly might indicate that you're bored or uninterested, while talking fast can mean you're excited or angry. It speaks to the energy you're exerting while in conversation.

- ✧ **Volume.** Talking loudly or softly. Again, talking loudly might mean you're fired up, excited, passionate, or angry. Talking softly can mean the conversation is more intimate or even private—or that you're just shy.

The way you combine all these elements will depend on the situation you're in, your mood, the environment, the people you're talking to, and so on. The way you talk to your sibling is different from the way you talk to your parents or a teacher, for example.

Verbal communication, simply put, is the physical act of conscious communication—you turn your internal dialogue into an external one. The type of language you use, along with clarity, tone, pitch, pace, and volume, are just tools you can use to effectively drive forth the intended meaning behind your words. The way you use these tools can also differ depending on who you're talking to and the circumstances surrounding the interaction.

Misunderstandings happen when the message you're trying to convey gets lost in translation somehow. This most often happens when there's a discrepancy between what you're saying and how you're saying it—or how you're using the different elements.

There are a lot of other things that affect how you present yourself to the world verbally, but this is the basics of verbal communication.

## Non-Verbal Communication

Non-verbal communication is how we send messages or convey information—either about ourselves or in reaction to others—through things like eye contact, body language, facial expressions, gestures, and even our appearance.

Did you know that 80% of communication happens non-verbally (Hull, 2016)? This means that the actual words that come out of your mouth only account for 20% of overall interaction. You could effectively have full-blown conversations with others without saying a single word.

Before we break down the elements of non-verbal communication, I want to talk a bit about first impressions. There's a famous quote from both Oscar Wilde and Will Rogers that you've likely heard by this point already: "You never get a second chance to make a first impression." (1966)

I mean… yes and no. From a literal standpoint, sure, you only get one shot at a first impression—unless the person forgot they met you in the first place. However, I think first impressions are overrated. You're going to tell me that you've never met someone, immediately didn't like them, but after spending some time with them, thought, *They're actually pretty cool?*

First impressions are a thing, but they don't hold nearly as much weight in casual everyday settings as people imply they do. Humans have a natural tendency to judge, and first impressions are a prime example of this. You can't possibly pretend to know me based on the first two minutes of meeting me (the average time "experts" say a first impression lasts). You can make judgments, assumptions, and form opinions, but once again, none of these are based on facts and all of it is subject to change over time.

I only bring this up to shed light on the fact that even if you mess up a first impression due to social anxiety, low confidence, or any other reason, you're not irredeemable; you're not doomed.

Here are the most important elements of non-verbal communication:

&#x2662; **Facial expressions.** You can tell a lot about what or how someone is feeling simply by looking at their face. Facial expressions for emotions can differ between cultures around the world, but the main ones (happiness, sadness, anger, and fear) are pretty universal and usually hard to hide.

✧ **Gestures.** These are any deliberate movements you use to add emotion or more influence behind your words, such as pointing, waving your hands around, rubbing your eyes, pinching the bridge of your nose, and so on. But it can also include things like giving someone a thumbs up, high-fiving, and so on.

✧ **Body language.** Your posture and subconscious body movements also signify your reaction or emotions. For example, crossing your arms is said to be a defensive gesture, fidgeting with something could indicate nervousness, and so on.

✧ **Eye contact.** Facial expression and emotion rely heavily on our eyes—they are the windows to the soul, after all. But they also play a big role in non-verbal communication through eye contact. Eye contact is important for establishing a connection.

✧ **Physical appearance.** It's not something we as a society should be proud of, but the way you look does have an impact on how people view and judge you. Your style is an extension of your personality, and by no means should you alter the way you dress or how you style your hair based on what other people may or may not think of you. The implication here is more on neatness and cleanliness. However, everyone has a different idea of what a neat and tidy appearance looks like—or should look like.

You don't need to be an expert on the theory of communication to communicate effectively. However, knowing the basics of verbal versus non-verbal communication can open up a whole new world where you're able to tell whether someone is authentic (their words match up with their behaviors) or being deceptive with malicious intent.

## Conversation Skills

My mom always said, "There's a difference between hearing and listening." And while I used to roll my eyes at the time, as an adult, I get it. What she really meant was there's a difference between simply listening to respond and listening to connect.

A conversation can be superficial. You don't have to form a deep and meaningful connection with the person who happens to be seated next to you on the bus or the guy who asks you if you know where the nearest bathroom is at the doctor's office. But if you are looking to start any type of long-lasting relationship with anyone, communication will be a big part of that.

There are four types of conversation:

⬥ **Discourse.** A one-way cooperative conversation where the purpose is to deliver information. A teacher presenting a lesson or presentation is a good example of this.

⬥ **Diatribe.** A one-way competitive conversation where the purpose is to inspire or express emotions (usually negative ones). An example of this is when your parents express concern over your latest test results.

✧ **Dialogue.** A cooperative two-way conversation where the purpose is to exchange information and build a relationship. For example, two friends discussing what they did over summer break, there's a back-and-forth exchange of questions and answers that spawn from genuine curiosity and interest.

✧ **Debate.** A competitive two-way conversation where the purpose is to win an argument or convince someone. You and your sibling disagree over which fast food restaurant has the best fries. You're arguing each other's reasonings and opinions in a way that's non-aggressive.

There's a time and place for each of these types of conversations; in fact, all of them are necessary depending on what you're trying to accomplish. They allow you to express your emotions, connect, and even disagree with people respectfully. That's the key word here: Respectfully.

I tend to agree with the phrase, "Respect is earned," but you can still lead with it and react accordingly. A rule I follow is that if I'm the one initiating contact or starting a conversation, I'm always respectful. Most of the time, people return the same energy, but I'm not going to continue being respectful if my respect is met with disrespect. And if someone comes up to me and doesn't lead with respect, I'm not wasting time or energy on the conversation because they clearly don't value me as a person.

There are some soft skills that come into play when engaging in conversation, most of which fall under verbal and non-verbal communication skills, such as eye contact, tone of voice, body language, yada, yada. But there are also things like active listening, reciprocity, social cues, and a host of other things that are important for engaging in a conversation and keeping others engaged as well.

We went over what verbal and non-verbal communication is—most of it is pretty straightforward and you probably understand and do most of it without trying already—but now we're going to break down the less obvious aspects of having a conversation and establishing a relationship.

### *Social Strategies*

Maybe your problem isn't actually with reading social cues but with initiating conversation and actually getting to a point where the interaction means something. You grasp the mechanics behind social interactions and have a good idea of how to participate, but it never seems to get past the small talk phase.

A good conversation is one that's pleasantly memorable; you wish you could've stayed longer, talked more, and can't wait to talk to them again. And yes, it's possible to feel all these feelings in regard to someone you don't necessarily want to pursue romantically.

You'd obviously feel more connected to someone who shares the same values, morals, and interests with you than you would with someone who doesn't. But that doesn't mean you can't form deep connections with someone who thinks differently than you. In fact, it's usually the people who bring up a different perspective that we might not have thought of that intrigues us.

Granted, if someone says something that you wholeheartedly disagree with, you might not want to be friends with them—and if they have extremely negative beliefs and values that are objectively immoral, you definitely shouldn't be. However, sometimes a good debate with someone who sees things in a different light is exhilarating and refreshing. If you only surround yourself with people who agree with you and never engage with people who don't, you risk being trapped in an echo chamber where you'll never be challenged to question yourself at all.

With that being said, there are some things that might be the cause for you not being able to hold a conversation or make it evolve into something deeper over time. Now, you might not even be aware that you're falling into these potholes, or it might not be something that's in your control, but keep in mind that you can work on improving them, which is the entire premise of this book:

- ✧ **Social anxiety.** Yes, yes, this isn't exactly new information. You've known about your social anxiety for a long time. But this *is* the most prominent reason for not being able to build or advance meaningful relationships.

Building a relationship with someone relies on your willingness to open up and be vulnerable. And with the probability of saying or doing something embarrassing being so high, you avoid it at all cost, which means avoiding social interaction altogether. The issue isn't in the act of doing or saying something embarrassing; it's in the fear surrounding it. You think you won't be able to redeem yourself after.

✧ **Fear of rejection.** Awkward moments and silences are a natural part of communication between one topic and the next—it's a turning point. No one likes awkward silences, but in your mind, it's a sign of rejection. And rejection is humiliating to most people.

Whether your cognitive distortions make you believe that someone is going to scoff in your face or flat-out ignore you when you try to talk to them, the fear of rejection is very real and can lead to social anxiety and, by extension, social withdrawal.

✧ **Lack of social skills.** Whether it's you not pulling your weight or them, a lack of social skills is a conversation extinguisher. It's hard to participate in a conversation when it seems like one of the participants is totally disengaged or uninterested.

Because that's what it looks like from the outside. Someone who lacks social skills may come across as rude when in reality, they just don't know what to say or how to reciprocate. Either way, it will lead to an abrupt end of any dialogue.

In order to have productive conversations that gradually evolve from generalized small talk to heart-to-heart personal deep dives, there are a few things to keep in mind. You're aiming for dialogue (from the four types of conversation), meaning that it's a two-way street, give and take. But how much is too much to give? How much is not enough?

Here are a few strategies and general guidelines to keep in mind and follow when talking to someone you really want to establish a continued relationship with:

- ✧ **Actively listening.** I don't mean just processing what someone is saying; I mean taking their facial expressions and body language into consideration as well as paying attention to what they're *not* saying. This prevents you from judging, jumping to conclusions, and assuming what other people are thinking or feeling.

  For example, if someone says, "Your hair looks different today," unless there's something in their tone of voice or body language that suggests they're trying to mock you, don't just assume they are. They simply made a statement.

  Actively paying attention to what someone is saying also includes not getting distracted by your phone or anything else and not interrupting them. This will help you remember what they're saying for future reference. You can also ensure you really understood what they were saying by rephrasing their words and asking clarifying questions if you're not sure that you're understanding correctly.

✧ **Ask open-ended questions.** Questions that can only be answered by a simple yes or no answer aren't the plague, and you don't have to recast or avoid asking a question entirely just because the answer is closed-ended. But you can follow it up with a question that requires a more elaborate answer. If someone says they've never heard of the band you like, ask them what type of music they're into and recommend a few songs from the band that fit that vibe.

And when someone asks you a yes or no type of question, try to add some additional yet relevant information. For example, if someone asks you if you like a certain band, instead of saying just yes or no, add on why you do or don't like them.

✧ **Be genuinely curious.** This kind of ties in with the previous bullet point, just on a much deeper level. Asking questions is a great way to get to know people, but showing genuine curiosity about other people's lives is more than that.

What I mean by being genuinely curious is, when they reveal something about themselves that you find interesting, don't just nod and say, "Oh, that's cool." Be curious! For example, let's say someone mentions that they dabble in music production; ask them if you can listen to some of their stuff, ask them how they got into it, what software they're using, how long they've been doing it, or if it's just a hobby or something they're serious about. Be excited for them, hype them up, and tell them if you're impressed.

However, don't force it. People can tell when you're being insincere. So this should only be done if and when you come across someone whose hobbies or skills you're truly fascinated by. Just make your curiosity apparent.

✧ **Relate.** Being able to relate to others is the most powerful way to form a connection. And this can happen in many aspects, but most commonly, it's similar or shared interests, hobbies, opinions, experiences, beliefs, and values. However, relating to someone doesn't guarantee a healthy, strong, or long-lasting relationship.

But it is a good way to open up a dialogue or initial conversation in order to figure out whether or not you are compatible. You might see someone drawing a character from your favorite anime series and you compliment them on their artistic talents. Maybe you become best friends, or maybe you realize after a while that besides having something in common, you don't really enjoy their company. But the only way to find out is to take that initial leap of faith.

✧ **Keep it light.** Don't reveal your deepest secrets or your entire life story in the first five minutes of introducing yourself. Small talk, although tedious and sometimes dull, is necessary. It can actually reveal a lot about you and the person you're talking to.

For instance, it can reveal whether someone has a good sense of humor, their communication style, or personality traits, and oftentimes provides us with useful information. So while small talk is usually about trivial, unimportant, or light-hearted topics, it lays the groundwork for future interactions.

You don't know them well enough to decide whether it's worth investing more time into the relationship. Small talk is limbo, in this case, a period of uncertainty as well as discovery.

And while you certainly can comment on the weather, there are also plenty of other menial topics to discuss: Movies, TV shows or series, music, and books; sporting events and championships, your favorite sports teams, exercise routines; favorite food, restaurants; culture; travel; celebrity gossip; hobbies and interests; family, where you grew up, the list goes one.

✧ **Go with it.** You don't—and shouldn't—do all the heavy lifting. Give the other person a chance to speak, ask questions, and reciprocate. Don't force abrupt subject changes and don't come on too strong with rapid-fire interrogational questions about their lives, hobbies, interests, and so on.

Let the conversation unfold naturally, and if a pause or awkward silence does inevitably happen, allow it to. Nothing is going to happen other than your brain making you hyper-aware that things are awkward right now. Building your tolerance to a point where you're able to endure the occasional awkward moment is a superpower!

Additionally, if you do get the vibe that someone might not be open to a conversation, don't take it personally, and don't force them into one. Don't keep on talking to someone if they aren't actively contributing for whatever reason.

- ✧ **Reflect.** Reflecting on the type and "quality" of the conversations you're currently having will help you improve your conversational skills and strategy. Think back on the conversations you've had over the past couple of days. How did you feel directly afterward? How did it start, and where did it end up? At which moments did it seem to be going well? What happened? Were there any moments where it seemed like it wasn't going well, and why do you think so?

The information from these questions might be able to give you an idea of what you're doing right, as well as areas that need improving. Be careful not to answer them with assumptions or negative beliefs, and be rational and realistic—look for evidence to confirm or deny your answers.

## Daily Task

There are many resources available that will help you improve your social skills, including books (like the one you're reading right now), podcasts, blogs, and worksheets. Your task for today is going to be broken up into a few simple steps that you might have to do over a period of time.

First, you're going to do some observing. Without changing anything about what you're doing during conversations today (or tomorrow if you're reading this late in the afternoon or right before bed), you're going to simply pay attention. Make notes after every social interaction if you're afraid you might forget things, such as others' reactions to something you did or said, your own reactions and body language, and so on.

At the end of the day, write down each area of social interaction that you believe you struggle with based on what sticks out to you (or your notes). Maybe it's reading and interpreting body language, active listening (or constantly interrupting people), taking part in group conversations, conflict resolution, and so on. It might help to ask for honest feedback from people who know you well, but try not to get discouraged or defensive when they list things you didn't even think or realize you do (or don't do). Though, you can also phrase the question as if you're asking for advice since some people might be afraid to offend you with a list of things you're doing "wrong."

Next, you're going to remind yourself that socializing is a skill and that you will improve with time and practice. Isolate one thing from your list of social skills that you can benefit from improving, and think of ways to do so. For example, if you find that you generally don't pay attention to people's facial expressions, challenge yourself to scan their faces every now and then and take in their expression at that specific moment (their eyebrows are raised, they're smiling, etc.). Even if you don't consciously know what it means, just noting or becoming aware of their facial expressions will give you a certain vibe.

Once you've improved that one area, then move on to the next one. Set small milestones and give yourself a pat on the back when you reach them.

You might have to do some additional research on social skills, cues, norms, and etiquette since I can't possibly cover everything there is to it in a single book, let alone a chapter, but you'll at least be able to get somewhere with what's covered here. And remember, perfection is overrated, not to mention subjective—aim for progress and you'll never fail.

CHAPTER 4

## Day 4    SOCIAL ANXIETY

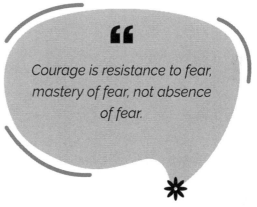

> *Courage is resistance to fear, mastery of fear, not absence of fear.*

–Mark Twain

✦✦✦✦

Humans are social creatures; we need connection and interaction to live a fulfilling life. Being afraid of rejection or embarrassment can definitely form part of social anxiety, but in its most severe form, it's a debilitating phobia that can present itself as physical symptoms like dizziness or full-blown panic attacks even during low-risk, casual, or fleeting interactions.

## Common Triggers

Social anxiety doesn't just randomly happen one Tuesday morning. There are lots of catalytic reasons for someone experiencing severe social anxiety, such as meeting new people, having to perform in front of a crowd, or fear of being embarrassed or humiliated. However, there's a difference between just experiencing nervousness and having social anxiety.

Social anxiety goes beyond being shy or feeling nervous in group settings or around people you don't know. Someone with a more severe form of social anxiety might go so far as to skip school, avoid grocery shopping, or cross the street when someone is about to walk past them on the sidewalk—they fear social situations *so* much that the mere thought of someone potentially greeting them is too much to bear.

Unsurprisingly, the root cause of severe or debilitating social anxiety is trauma (either domestic or social) related to negative past experiences such as having been bullied, teased, rejected, ridiculed, abandoned, and abused. Typically, the symptoms of social anxiety start in early childhood, but it's also possible to develop it later in life as a teenager or even as an adult.

Having social anxiety usually interferes with every aspect of a person's daily life and their ability to function normally. They don't simply get jittery right before they give a speech; they have sleepless nights about it for weeks or even months in advance. They worry about potentially being in a situation where they have to communicate with others—and they will go out of their way to avoid it at all costs.

It is possible to overcome social anxiety, but know that it will require you to face your fears (in small, manageable increments) and build up a tolerance to your triggers and reactions. And that is exactly what we'll be going over in this chapter. And even if you don't have social anxiety, these techniques could still be useful for putting yourself out there if you struggle with nervousness or shyness.

## Managing Symptoms

The whole reason why social anxiety makes it so hard to function is because of the symptoms. A trigger sets off your fight or flight response, which makes your body pump out adrenaline like it's going out of style. This leads to physical symptoms such as shortness of breath, upset stomach (nausea or an intense feeling of "butterflies" that doesn't go away within seconds), shaky voice or hands, tight chest, fast heart rate, sweating or hot flashes, and feeling dizzy or faint. All of these symptoms, stacked on top of the mental aspects of social anxiety, could cause a full nervous system meltdown, resulting in a panic attack.

It's automatic and unavoidable; every fiber in your being is screaming at you to run because the situation is dangerous— even if you consciously know that's not true most of the time. By re-regulating your nervous system when the involuntary fight or flight response kicks in, you reduce the symptoms. And by reducing the symptoms, you're better able to face the fear and eventually even overcome it.

A few ways you can re-regulate your nervous system and manage the physical manifestations of social anxiety in the moment are as follows:

- ✧ **Breathing and relaxation exercises.** This is arguably the most effective way to relieve the uncomfortable and alarming symptoms of social anxiety quickly. All there is to it is taking a big breath in (the deepest you can manage) and slowly breathing out. Try to elongate the time it takes to breathe in and out with each breath, so start with two seconds per breath and work your way up to ten seconds or longer. While you do this, try to become aware of some areas or muscle groups where the tension might be residing (the jaw, shoulders, hips, etc.), and focus on releasing it. Picture the tension leaving your body as you exhale.

  You might have to excuse yourself if you're feeling really overwhelmed and do this in a bathroom or somewhere else that's private, but you can also do it on the spot if you feel comfortable enough to do so.

- ✧ **Grounding.** A common tactic usually used in people who are on the verge of an anxiety or panic attack, but it works for social anxiety as well. It's called the 5-4-3-2-1 coping technique and it requires you to (when you feel dysregulated or overwhelmed) name five things you can see, four things you can touch, three things you can hear, two things you can smell, and one thing you can taste.

The goal of this exercise is to bring you back to the present moment instead of letting the panic or fear take over and progressively worsen.

✧ **Challenge your thoughts.** Break down your thoughts and fears and, using logic and objectivity, debunk them or challenge them. In the case of social anxiety, negative thoughts and fears are usually rooted in doing or saying something that you believe others might judge or ridicule you for. More on this later.

✧ **Acknowledge your symptoms.** Admitting to yourself what you're feeling and how these emotions are physically showing up in your body can bring comfort and relief in and of itself—to some degree. This could look like thinking something as simple as, "I am feeling really anxious right now because I'm about to talk to someone I don't know," or "There's a pit in my stomach and I feel dizzy because of my social anxiety."

You could also pair this with some form of reassurance phrase or affirmation like "I'm not in danger" or "This feeling will pass; just breathe."

Relieving symptoms of social anxiety in stressful situations is very helpful, but there are also some lifestyle changes you can make that will reduce your social anxiety in general and in the long term:

- ✧ **Diet and exercise.** Dietary changes don't have to be drastic or restrictive. Even small changes like limiting caffeine while making sure you're adding protein, fiber, and fruits or vegetables to most daily meals can make a difference.

  Exercise includes any form of movement, bonus points if it's actually something you enjoy doing, like hiking (or just taking a walk), totem tennis (swingball), or jumping on a trampoline. It doesn't have to include repetitive movements, weight lifting, or excessive sweating. Increased activity not only takes your mind off of the things making you anxiously overthink, but it also decreases long-term muscle tension and encourages the production of stress-relieving hormones. It even helps you manage future nervous system reactions to perceived threats, meaning that it literally helps you deal with triggers relating to social anxiety (Ratey, 2019).

- ✧ **Sleep.** It's hard to get a good night's sleep if you have social anxiety, and ironically, a lack of sleep (or sleep deprivation) actually worsens your symptoms of social anxiety—it also takes a toll on your general mental and physical health.

  Sleep deprivation or difficulties with sleep that persist and don't improve when you're taking measures to reduce overall anxiety should always be taken seriously and checked out by a medical professional.

✧ **Meditation.** There's a lot of debate about what meditation really is and how it should be done. I'm here to tell you that, once again, there are no rules. If the way you approach it works, it's worth doing.

Now, there are many ways to meditate, some more serious than others. But you don't have to be sitting cross-legged, eyes closed, with your thumb and middle finger touching on your knees for hours to benefit from it. Meditation is simply the act of focused concentration and staying in the present moment. You pick something neutral to focus on (like your breathing, a phrase or mantra, the texture on the wall, or your movements) and you stay there for a bit—as long as you need to.

Your mind will get bored and wander; when this happens, you gently nudge it back to whatever your neutral focal point is. You can also adapt this so you're focusing intently on whatever mundane tasks you're doing, like walking, brushing your teeth, packing the dishwasher, and so on. Feel the pebbles crunching under your feet, the smell of the rose bush you're passing, and hear the wind rushing past you. Feel the coolness of the minty toothpaste in your mouth, taste it, the circular motions of the bristles. Just pay attention to life!

Meditation works to reduce symptoms of anxiety by reducing or eliminating mind clutter and slowing your thoughts so you can process emotions and experiences better. It puts you into a deep state of relaxation which results in a feeling of peace and harmony between mind and body. And this state of practiced tranquility becomes almost like muscle memory which you can pull from during stressful times. It's a healthy and effective long-term coping mechanism.

✧ **Therapy.** If your social anxiety is severe and nothing you try to implement or do is helping in any capacity, seeking professional help is the only remaining option. A licensed therapist or counselor will provide more specialized and personal insight into your situation. They will work with you to build the tools and skills necessary to overcome social anxiety and even help you find the right medications if needed.

✧ **Positive affirmations.** Yes, I know I've mentioned this before; I'm telling you again for good reason. Positive affirmations are a popular cognitive behavioral therapy tool used to treat mental disorders such as depression and anxiety. It involves looking in the mirror and rehearsing a list of nice things about yourself. And while it sounds silly and embarrassing, it has a surprisingly high success rate—the mind is a very powerful thing.

Do you know why positive affirmations work so well? Because if you tell yourself something over and over again, eventually, you'll believe it. But this works in reverse, too. Meaning that negative voice in your head that has been there since you can remember has been bamboozling you this entire time!

This is also how your brain creates biases. When you don't see yourself as worthy of love, respect, friendship, or support, you're less likely to value your existence and your contributions. You don't see why there's a need to look after yourself, so you don't. You think no one would value you, not because of their actions, but because, in your mind, you're not worth the effort in the first place. Every small and potentially innocent gesture from someone else gets twisted in your mind and serves as further evidence that you're simply not enough.

## Overcoming Social Anxiety

I don't know if you've ever looked at a word and thought you misspelled it. And then you look it up and you actually didn't, but it still looks wrong. It's called "wordnesia" and the psychology behind it is interesting. When we read, we don't focus on the individual letters; rather, our brains automatically interpret it as a unit (i.e., a word). But when you become hyper-focused on the individual letters, you temporarily lose the ability to see the word as a whole. So, in your mind, it's no longer a word you recognize, if that makes any sense.

My hypothesis is that this is more or less what happens when you hyper-focus on a specific trait, attribute, or feature of yourself. Your brain blows it out of proportion and you're left with the result: anxiety.

The first step to overcoming social anxiety is to identify your triggers, and the second step is to find the techniques that help reduce the symptoms in both the short and long term. But in order to overcome it, you will have to face it. Unfortunately, there's no way around this one. In fact, the more you avoid your triggers, emotional reactions, and physical symptoms, the stronger they get.

Avoiding the things that cause an adverse negative physical and emotional response within us is encoded into our DNA. It's as much a part of you as the color of your eyes and the thickness of your fingernails are. It's a survival instinct.

### Challenge Your Beliefs

The only constant in life is change. Your thoughts, beliefs, assumptions, and expectations are always changing. Or at least, it should. That's why public opinion, laws, legislation, and the status quo have continuously changed over the course of human history. Because we are constantly learning and discovering new information through studies, philosophers, and medicine. Because it's good to question things, consider alternative perspectives, outcomes, impacts, and decide to do better–be better.

We can look at some ideologies of our ancestors, the beliefs and behaviors that were considered "normal" in those times and grimace. We use that knowledge and information to change the way we do things, the way we see things, and we use it to literally change the world!

But won't actively challenging every thought and belief you have cause even more self-doubt and therefore lower your self-esteem even further? No, but it is a slippery slope. *Challenging* your beliefs (if you're going about it the right way) can strengthen and change your opinions and worldview for the better. *Overthinking* it can lead to mind clutter and self-doubt.

This is why I'm going to tell you how you should go about challenging your thoughts in a way that stops the cycle in its tracks instead of just branching off, making everything worse.

What is the difference between knowledge and belief? Knowledge requires evidence; it's rooted in reality; it's objective. Belief is conceptual knowledge, a strongly held opinion, meaning that even though something might be true, it can't be backed up with proof, and–more often than not—it's subjective (it can be influenced by thoughts, emotions, and assumptions).

An example that might help differentiate the two can be as simple as this: Imagine you're at a store, and you know this store very well. Based on your *knowledge*, you know they have cool ranch Doritos because you physically see it on the shelf, you can pick it up, and you can rip open the bag and eat it (assuming you're going to pay for it). However, that's not to say they're going to have it in stock the next time you come to this exact store. You may *believe* they have it based on your past experiences of buying it, but that doesn't necessarily make it true.

Being able to identify whether a thought is actual knowledge or just a belief is important because it will help you sift through your inner dialogue to find the limiting or negative beliefs that should be challenged in the first place.

Let's take a singular limiting belief that you may or may not have on a regular basis and go through the process of challenging it together. You can obviously swap out the context of the belief if you already have a different one in mind at this moment.

The limiting belief is: "No one likes me; that's why I have no friends."

**Step 1: Pause.** Let the thought resonate for a second. Really consider the words, the implications it has had on you, and the consequences.

**Step 2: Determine whether it's knowledge or belief.** Correlation doesn't equal causation. Ask yourself questions about your belief, such as: What proof do you have that this thought is objectively true? Can you read minds? Has every person you've ever met outright told you that they didn't like you, or is it merely a conclusion you drew based on their behavior? Just because you have no friends doesn't automatically mean it's because no one likes you.

**Step 3: Consider the alternatives.** Could it be possible that maybe people don't interact with you as much because you seem standoffish due to your belief that no one likes you? Could it be possible that other people are unsure of you because your fear of judgment makes it so you never reveal who you truly are? Could it be that your unwillingness to be vulnerable makes you look unapproachable?

**Step 4: Gather new evidence.** Now that you're considering alternative reasons for your belief, determine which ones are actually true. Think back to when you were in a setting where your belief seemed to be stronger than ever and find proof that supports the alternative reasons for the belief. Using our example, you can try to remember (in as much detail as you can) what your body language was like. Were you huddled in a corner, too scared to join the conversation? Were there opportunities to join the conversion that you didn't take? Did others maybe try to get you to join in by asking questions but your responses were short and detached? Did you maybe seem disinterested and only gave one-sided responses without throwing questions back at them?

**Step 5: Experiment.** You can test out your new-found beliefs and theories to solidify them. The next time the opportunity presents itself, change one small thing in the way you approach the situation and see if it makes any difference or supports your alternative belief. With our example, you can be more engaged in a group conversation by nodding along, expressing opposing opinions, and asking questions. Even if you're not in a group discussion, maybe you overhear someone say something to someone else that interests you and you—politely—pipe in with a question, statement, or simply agree with the person.

**Step 6: Move on to the next limiting belief.** Don't try to conquer all your limiting beliefs at once, as this can be overwhelming. It might take some time, practice, and courage, but one by one, you'll discover, debunk, and rectify the limiting beliefs that are holding you back in life. And even make a few friends along the way.

Focus on breaking down complex thoughts into one sentence and then deconstruct them using the steps outlined above. Write down your limiting beliefs as well as the process of dissecting and rationalizing them; when you try to do it in your head, things can get jumbled or spiral into different directions resulting in overthinking and additional mind clutter.

It could also help to start with thoughts that are a little less triggering and also do it while you're in a neutral headspace. Trying to change your perspective is hard on a good day, so make sure you're able to confront uncomfortable truths that come from challenging your thoughts. It could also help going over this process with someone you trust and who won't judge you; they could even answer some questions you may be stuck on or help you uproot personal biases (we all have them and it can be hard to spot them ourselves).

In the beginning, challenging a thought can feel forced or inauthentic. Like you're gaslighting yourself. But that's the thing; the whole reason challenging your thoughts is necessary is because you gaslit yourself into a limiting belief in the first place!

Try to give your mind some time to process all the new information and epiphanies that come up after challenging a belief. Do something that temporarily distracts you, like playing a video game for a couple of hours, helping your mom with dinner, or playing with a pet.

## Exposure Therapy

How do you overcome a literal disorder that makes you believe and react as though making small talk with a stranger is equivalent to coming face-to-face with a grizzly bear? You slowly convince your brain that the threat is not as severe as it thinks or believes it to be.

It's called gradual exposure therapy or systematic desensitization. What it does is build your tolerance to triggers and emotional reactions by facing something, starting with the least fear-inducing situation and working your way up once you're ready and comfortable.

Basically, taking itty-bitty steps at a time and making gradual progress. Gradual exposure therapy is used in conjunction with relaxation techniques to help you stay regulated during the entire process.

The goal of gradual exposure therapy is to condition you or to help you build resilience so you're able to eventually face your fears—or in this case, social anxiety—without getting overwhelmed or inducing a panic attack which can be very traumatic and worsen your fear.

When implementing this desensitization technique, it helps to think of your fear in terms of levels. A level one fear is something that makes you feel the least amount of discomfort or anxiety, and obviously, a level ten fear would be something that causes the most adverse reaction.

The first step is to identify your personal level one and level ten fear. For example, a level one fear might be raising your hand in class, and a level ten fear is being at a party surrounded by mostly strangers and not knowing what to do with yourself (just the thought of it makes your stomach flip).

The next step is to identify all the levels of fear between one and ten. So level two could be seeing someone you know in public, level three is meeting someone new, and so on. The levels of fear get progressively more anxiety-inducing. Once you have your list, phase two can commence. Phase two is when you start exposing yourself to those fears in a controlled way.

What I mean by facing your fears in a controlled way is imagining a scenario of your fear taking place and then keeping yourself calm with your preferred breathing or relaxation technique as you do it. Rinse and repeat until the thought of your level-one fear no longer induces a physical or emotional reaction anymore.

Only once you're able to visualize or imagine yourself doing the thing you fear while being able to stay calm do you move on to real life. Using the example of a level one fear being raising your hand in class, the next time the opportunity presents itself, try to calm your nerves and do it. If the anxiety gets too bad and you're unable to keep calm and actually do it in the moment, it's okay! Go back to simply visualizing it while practicing your calming technique. Try again when you feel ready to.

Eventually, you'll do your level one fear for the first time. Then you'll do it more confidently, and then you'll do it without fear at all. At that point, you're done; you've overcome your level-one fear. Now you'll repeat this process for your level two fear until you reach level ten.

Some fears, however, might be hard or illogical to try and face or recreate in real life. For example, falling down or tripping in front of people. Please don't purposely trip or fall. Instead, what you can do is stick to the visualization practice while practicing staying calm, and if it does happen at some point, try to remember your training. Just breathe; it's going to be fine.

## Daily Task

Gradual exposure therapy is, as the name suggests, gradual. Meaning it can take weeks—if not longer—until you're able to face a single fear in real life. So your task for today is to graze against the boundaries of your comfort zone in other areas of your life that may not be directly related to your social anxiety.

Stepping out of your comfort zone will translate or bleed into other areas and build your confidence and self-esteem. Get creative with it. Here's a list of things you can do to push the boundaries of what you're comfortable with (in a good way). Challenge yourself to do one of them today, or pick a few and do all of them over the span of a month:

- ✧ Take a cold shower.
- ✧ Change the route you take to school.
- ✧ Visit a new place (park, street, shopping center, etc.).
- ✧ Write using your non-dominant hand.
- ✧ Listen to a song you've never heard before (or don't like).
- ✧ Try out a new recipe.
- ✧ Go vegan for the day (if you're not already).
- ✧ Film yourself dancing or practicing a skill.

- ✧ Take a picture of yourself every day for a month.

- ✧ Change up your morning, evening, or workout routine.

- ✧ Ditch social media for a day.

- ✧ Start that creative project you've been meaning to do.

- ✧ Rearrange your room furniture.

- ✧ Sit in a place you've never sat before (a different couch, an ottoman, or a specific spot on the floor).

- ✧ Pick up a new skill or interest.

- ✧ Do something differently from how you've been doing it before.

- ✧ Change the scent of your shampoo, deodorant, lotion, body spray, or perfume.

- ✧ Order something you've never had before from a restaurant or fast food joint.

- ✧ Introduce yourself to a stranger (who you'll likely never see again).

- ✧ Reach out to someone you've fallen out of touch with or haven't spoken to in a while.

- ✧ Take on volunteer work that has to do with interacting with other humans.

- ✧ Eat at a restaurant by yourself.

- ✧ Ask someone for a recommendation (their favorite book, movie, or video game, for example).

- ✧ Sign up for a group class or extracurricular activity that you think you might enjoy.

✧ Give someone a compliment.

✧ Tell someone you know how much you appreciate them.

✧ Invite a classmate you don't know that well over to your house.

Get comfortable with change, tension, awkwardness, and the unknown. Someone once said, "If it doesn't challenge you, it doesn't change you." The only certainty in life is uncertainty; once you're able to laugh in the face of discomfort, you can take on the world!

# CONNECTION

✦ ✦ ✦ ✦

All the small talk in the world isn't enough to establish a genuine, deep, and meaningful connection with someone. That's because the connection is based on mutual respect, trust, commitment, interest, and value. All of these are difficult to accomplish when you have social anxiety, lack certain social skills, or have some form of past trauma or negative experiences that you feel you need to actively protect yourself from.

Again, it's not your fault, but it is your responsibility to improve yourself, learn, and heal from your past. You can't force deeper connections with people, but you can place yourself in a position where it's more likely to happen.

## Empathy and Understanding

Empathy is an interpersonal skill that involves being able to recognize, understand, and relate to others and their emotions and behaviors, even if you may think they're being dramatic or overreacting. It allows you to support others through certain situations and make them feel better.

Just because you're not afraid of frogs doesn't mean there aren't people who find them terrifying. A person with empathy isn't going to shame or belittle someone else for reacting differently than they themselves would've.

The difference between empathy and sympathy is understanding and shared experience. You feel sympathy if you see a stranger crying and empathy if you can relate to why they're crying (and you feel the need to support them in some capacity). So while sympathy can certainly turn into empathy, ultimately, they are separate things.

There are three stages of empathy:

1. **Cognitive empathy.** When you can identify someone else's emotional state (you see them crying and recognize that they are sad).

2. **Emotional empathy.** The ability to share or engage with the emotions of others (their emotions affect your own).

3. **Compassionate empathy.** When you actively try to reduce the emotional turmoil of others (you ask what's wrong or try to cheer them up).

There should obviously be some boundaries around the amount of empathy you are capable of showing at certain times. If you are going through a rough time, you can't always be there and support others to the best of your abilities. But empathy, along with body language awareness, does play a big part in human connection—and it should be reciprocated.

## *Body Language Awareness*

I feel like it's appropriate to start with being able to read someone's body language or at least be aware of it and what it might indicate. It's important to note that reading body language is not an accurate way of determining someone's thoughts or feelings. Many people take reading body language way too seriously.

Reading body language is subjective, and a lot of the meanings overlap or even contradict each other. What I mean by this is that someone could scratch their nose, which, in body language lingo, means they're being insincere or dishonest when in reality, they just had an itchy nose at the wrong moment. For this reason, you should never 100% rely on body language alone to try and figure out what others are thinking or feeling.

Here's a breakdown of the most common body language cues and what they could potentially mean when they happen during a conversation:

- ✧ **Eye contact.** There's no correct amount of eye contact to give or receive. Too much eye contact can leave you or the other person feeling uncomfortable, and too little might mean you or the other person is distracted, uncomfortable, uninterested, or trying to hide true thoughts or feelings. The eyebrows are also typically pretty involved with emotions. For example, upturned eyebrows (think cartoon-style sadness) only happen during genuine sadness, empathy, or concern and are hard to replicate without real emotion tied to it (unless you're Amelia Clark, she manages to pull this off quite flawlessly).

- ✧ **The mouth.** Pursed lips usually signal disagreement, disapproval, or disgust. Lip biting could mean the person is stressed or anxious, and covering one's mouth can be a way to hide certain emotions from showing. Then there's the obvious: smiling. A genuine smile is one that "reaches the eyes," which is just code for when the eyes are engaging in it as well (narrowing and creasing in the outer corners). When the eyes are not actively participating in the smile, it could mean that the person is just trying to be polite; it doesn't mean that they're being fake—especially if they do this when they don't really know you very well.

✧ **Hands, arms, and legs.** Crossed arms or legs can be an indication that someone is defensive, dismissive, or disinterested. While clasping one's hands behind the back could signal boredom. Fidgeting is typically a sign that someone is nervous, frustrated, or impatient. Clenched fists signify unity or anger. Personal space also goes hand-in-hand with this; the more space a person takes up, the more confidence they tend to have. But if they're invading your personal space, it could mean they're trying to intimidate you.

✧ **Posture.** This is how a person holds themselves in a general sense. A closed-off posture (hunched over, taking up the least amount of space possible, crossed arms or legs, avoiding eye contact) could mean someone is generally an anxious or anti-social person (or they're just shy and uncomfortable), while an open posture (body takes up the necessary space, arms and legs are relaxed, the torso is exposed, not avoiding eye contact) typically indicates that someone is more confident and willing to engage in friendly conversation.

Again, I want to reiterate that body language is not the end-all-be-all of dissecting what someone might be thinking or feeling. However, if someone's words are not lining up with their body language, that is—more often than not—a sign that they are not really someone to be trusted. Chances are your subconscious will pick up on this anyway and your instincts will warn you of this to some degree.

The body language or "social cues" explained above are only the metaphorical tip of the iceberg. Don't get too caught up in learning everything there is to know about body language and using only that to figure people out. Body language is just too complicated, ambiguous, and multifactorial to rely on accurately.

## Healthy Relationships

Relationships, whether it be romantic, platonic, or familial, enrich our lives and fulfills our need for belonging, support, and love. But not all relationships are created equal, some look, feel, and function differently than others. The important thing is that any relationship you cultivate should be healthy and happy.

This doesn't mean that you'll never argue, disagree, or unintentionally hurt each other, but it does mean you're able to respectfully and reasonably work it out and return to equilibrium.

But how do you know whether a relationship is healthy or not?

A healthy relationship is one where both or all parties involved are mutually supportive, trusting, accepting, supportive of personal growth, and adaptable to change. Overall, it *feels* good. You're never left questioning whether or not this person's intentions or behaviors are real and virtuous.

## *How To Spot a Toxic Person*

The best cure is prevention. Toxic people will drain the life out of you, and while it isn't always possible to avoid interacting with toxic people, you definitely want to avoid giving off the impression that you're open to it.

General signs that someone might be toxic include selfish, hostile, and manipulative behavior. But here are a few more specific traits or behaviors that a toxic person might exhibit:

- always negative
- quick to judge
- lies and deceives
- general rudeness
- lack of empathy
- always thinks the worst of others
- being reckless
- argumentative
- gets aggressive or goes on the offense very easily
- controlling
- self-centered
- arrogant
- greedy
- disruptive or spiteful
- impulsivity

✧ apathy

✧ selfishness

✧ perfectionistic

It's important to remember that our actions don't always define who we are, but recurring negative themes and behaviors from people without taking accountability usually means they lack self-awareness. And without self-awareness, they won't change—or even admit that they're the problem in the first place.

Bear in mind that toxic traits can also exist within ourselves, so if you relate a bit too much to some of what was mentioned here, you're not a bad person. As long as you're willing to take accountability for it and work on changing for the better, you're already doing more than most people are!

### How To Build Healthy Relationships

If you're someone who's particularly withdrawn, shy, or has social anxiety, building true, deep, and meaningful relationships has probably been a struggle for as long as you can remember. The truth is relationships of any nature are hard to grow and take effort to maintain, like a well-manicured garden.

Your garden might look sparse and overgrown right now, but once you take care of the soil (build self-esteem and social skills) and trim back the weeds (overcome social anxiety or fear), something is bound to sprout if you sow the right seeds and remember to water it every now and then.

Here's how to cultivate relationships and build connections that last:

- ✧ **Be authentic from the start.** If you're the type of person who is always looking for validation or approval from others (in other words, a people pleaser), it might be challenging to break out of this behavior. But pretending to be someone you're not so others would like you is simply not sustainable. Eventually, you'll burn out. Not to mention the other person might feel confused or betrayed because your behavior is inconsistent, which leads to distrust and suspicion on their end.

  Fight the urge to pretend you like something, know something, or believe something you don't. Avoid acting in a way that doesn't feel true to who you are.

- ✧ **Be thoughtful and empathetic.** It can be awkward or uncomfortable when someone shares something deeply intimate or personal with you. Unless they specifically ask for advice, don't give any. Sometimes people just need to vent, and someone venting to you is usually a good sign that they trust you. Simply acknowledging their feelings with a "that sucks, I'm so sorry" or "I don't know what to say, but I'm here for you" is all that's necessary. Thank them for sharing their feelings with you because it usually takes a lot of courage to do so.

Being thoughtful can look like a lot of things, but paying attention and being present in a conversation to pick up what they might like or dislike is a good start. Not only can it give you a pretty good idea of what to get them for their birthdays, but it shows you really care about what they're saying and that they're important to you.

◇ **Be reliable.** Following through with promises or commitments you make to someone lets them know you're someone who can be trusted, and trust is a very important element of any relationship. This doesn't mean there won't be times when you have to cancel plans or tend to something urgent that came up instead, but being upfront and honest about it when it happens is key to maintaining any trust you've built.

◇ **Set boundaries.** Boundaries are like invisible lines— usually regarding behavior, but they can also apply to more ambiguous aspects—that you enforce in any relationship. It's like personal expectations and limitations.

Boundaries allow all parties to feel safe and comfortable, and adhering to each other's boundaries is a sign of mutual respect. Having boundaries is non-negotiable, and being able to both communicate your own and respect the other person's is the epitome of a healthy relationship.

Someone might question your boundaries, and you can certainly discuss why you have that boundary in a respectful way (if you feel comfortable doing so), but if someone judges, protests, or outright ignore it the first chance they get, that's a telltale sign that someone is toxic.

✧ **Communicate.** Okay, duh! Obviously, if you want to build a relationship with someone, it will require some form of continued communication. But bonding with someone isn't going to happen at a constant rate. Some moments will be raw and vulnerable, and others might be more superficial.

Enjoy the good moments because those make the best memories, lean into the vulnerability when it happens, and communicate openly when there are issues or tension for whatever reason.

It goes without saying that all of the points mentioned above should be reciprocated or mutual. Relationships are give-and-take, sometimes compromises are warranted and life happens. Don't be afraid to be vulnerable and express your feelings; in the grand scheme of things, it's unlikely that you'll ever regret it.

## Respectful Expression

Everyone has their own idea of what respect means. The official definition of respect as a noun in the Merriam-Webster dictionary is: "To consider worthy of high regard." And, not surprisingly, that description is pretty spot on.

The way I define respect for myself is by treating others like human beings regardless of their age, race, culture, health, or status because we all have intrinsic value. The only thing that can influence my respect for others is a lack of reciprocity thereof.

I once saw a Tumblr post (yes, I'm that old) where someone compared the respect of personhood to the respect of authority. What it basically said was that people share this ideology of respect, meaning: If you treat me like a person, I'll treat you like a person. But there are some people—usually people in power—who, when they talk about mutual respect, really mean: Only if you treat me like an authority will I treat you like a person. And that has really stuck with me.

Entitled people aside, respect is a virtue that we all have the ability to grant to others. It builds trust, prevents conflict, and shows emotional intelligence and maturity. This doesn't mean that you'll never be in situations where someone is disrespectful to you or that you should never disagree with someone. But disagreeing with someone and being able to express your thoughts and feelings in a respectable way is an important skill to have in all forms of relationships.

Unless someone is just an awful or immature person, being respectful when setting boundaries, calling them out for their behavior, and disagreeing will actually strengthen a relationship. And knowing how to deal with receiving disrespect can help you feel more confident and assertive—you deserve respect, don't settle for less.

Here's how to express your opinions, thoughts, needs, and emotions in a respectful manner:

- ✧ **Be assertive.** You can express yourself confidently and respectfully at the same time. And yes, this will take practice. You have to believe that you're worth standing up for and realize that the only person who's going to stand up for you *is* you. People can't read your mind, which is why you have to tell them when they've said or done something that has hurt you, or when you disagree with them, or when they're being unfair or rude.

  Being assertive doesn't mean you should be aggressive, rude, confrontational, or disrespectful. It means you value yourself and your rights while also acknowledging the rights of others. It's about being fair to yourself and others regardless of how they might react to it.

- ✧ **Reframe the statement.** When you want to express your needs, thoughts, opinions, or emotions, outright telling someone that they are the reason you feel a certain type of way can cause them to feel attacked. This might lead them to become defensive or even start an argument, and that will not yield productive results. Your goal isn't to argue but to resolve.

Instead, you can reframe your statement. So, instead of saying, "You always expect me to drop everything and clean my room when you tell me to," you can say, "I feel frustrated when you tell me to clean my room when I'm busy. I know it needs to be done; can I do it later?"

✧ **Understand their point of view.** We're quick to disagree with someone if they're doing or saying something we don't approve of. But unless they're being rude or disrespectful, take a moment to process whatever it is that you don't agree with. Try to see things from their perspective, taking into consideration what information is or isn't available to them.

If you still can't understand where they're coming from, you can tell them how and why you disagree without attacking or making fun of them for their views and opinions.

✧ **Be considerate.** Talk to people the way you want to be talked to. Again, this doesn't mean that others will return the favor. However, a hallmark sign of being emotionally mature and respectful is leading by example. By considering the other person's feelings, you can prevent them from lashing out and causing an argument.

There are ways to go about expressing your feelings, thoughts, or opinions without being rude or judgmental. Some people will defend their direct rudeness or disrespect by saying they're "brutally" honest. I find that to be a lame excuse; you can be honest while still being kind and considerate.

For example, let's say someone you're talking to has something stuck in their teeth; the only options here are telling them or ignoring it. Not telling them isn't the kind thing to do, in my opinion. Think of it this way, if you had something stuck in your teeth, would you prefer it if someone told you or left you to go the whole day without knowing?

Being considerate is all in the delivery. Saying, "Oh, you have something in your teeth," without making a big deal out of it versus pulling a face and saying, "Ew, what's in your teeth?" Both scenarios display honesty, but only one is being considerate.

## Daily Task

I get it. It seems daunting and scary to meet new people. Not every person you meet will become a permanent or important fixture in your life, and there's no way to know which relationships are built to last. But that's the name of the game; life is just one big gamble, really.

But you can't let the uncertainty stop you from trying, and you can't let the fear of wasting your time and effort stop you from participating at all. And you can't let your fear of rejection, embarrassment, or awkward moments dictate everything you do for the rest of your life. So here's what you're going to do today:

You're going to make micro-commitments. These are low-risk, medium-reward actions that might or might not result in an opportunity to get to know someone just a bit better, such as:

- ✧ Add someone from your friend recommendation lists to Snapchat, Facebook, or Instagram.

- ✧ Greet someone when they walk past you.

- ✧ Give someone a genuine compliment (their shoes, an accessory, their outfit, or skills are all safe options to go for).

- ✧ Ask to borrow something, but remember to give it back (an eraser, a pencil, white-out, etc.).

- ✧ Make that comment, either on social media or in real life, given that it's polite and appropriate (bonus points if it's funny).

- ✧ Ask someone for their opinion or recommendation.

- ✧ Agree (or disagree) with someone—respectfully, of course.

A lot of things can be an opportunity to start or join in on a conversation; you just have to take a chance sometimes. People are like flavors, some complement each other, and some don't mix, but it takes a certain level of risk and experimentation to figure it out.

CHAPTER 6

# Day 6

# HANDLING DIFFICULT SOCIAL SITUATIONS

> **"**
>
> *I am not afraid of storms for I am learning how to sail my ship.*

✼

*–Louise May Alcott*

✦ ✦ ✦ ✦

No matter what you do, there will always be conflict in any relationship. In fact, conflict is a sign of a healthy relationship. People have this idea that conflict is a bad thing that should be avoided. But that's simply not true. No two people are going to see eye to eye on everything all the time. It highlights the beautiful uniqueness that exists within all of humanity.

That being said, conflict isn't a sign that two people are incompatible, and it's how you handle the conflict that matters. It can strengthen and help the relationship grow, or it can burn it to the ground.

Conflict resolution is a necessary soft skill that is unimaginably important in most areas of your life, both now and in the future. You will use it with your future romantic partner, your colleagues, your boss, your friends, and even your children (if you decide to have them).

## What Is Conflict?

Conflict is more than a disagreement. However, disagreements can certainly turn into conflict if it's not resolved properly. Conflict is a situation where someone feels threatened or becomes emotionally triggered due to the actions or words of someone else (usually someone they consider a friend, but can also be an acquaintance or stranger).

It doesn't go away when you ignore it. In fact, unresolved conflict will only become worse over time. And as crazy as it sounds, conflict is an opportunity to build trust and security in the relationship, but that will depend on your (and the other person's) ability to overcome it.

Your perception of conflict will tell you a lot about your conflict resolution skills. For example, if you're the type of person who avoids arguments, doesn't uphold your own boundaries, or defends or ignores others' negative actions toward you instead of bringing it up to them, you're probably not very good at it—no offense.

But you have to admit it makes perfect sense; if a person avoids conflict at all costs, then that means they haven't had much (if any) experience dealing with it. Hence, their problem-solving abilities go down the drain or never develop fully in the first place.

The good news is it's never too late to learn.

## Conflict Resolution

How you handle conflict comes down to your ability to stay calm and alert when emotions are running high. This means that even when someone has said or done something that has triggered an adverse emotional response, you're able to re-regulate and continue to engage and even face the conflict head-on.

There are two main skills of conflict resolution: Emotional awareness and emotional regulation.

Staying calm during a stressful time allows you to still be aware of social cues and body language so you can assess the situation properly. It's important to regulate your emotions during conflict, so you're able to communicate your needs and feelings in a way that won't escalate things but rather resolve them.

## Strategies

There are five main strategies for resolving conflict, but they're not all equal and the method you choose will depend on the importance, impact, and consequences it will have on everyone involved. The five conflict resolution strategies are:

✧ **Avoidance.** This is when you try to sidestep or ignore the issue at hand. And while it's not recommended in most situations, there are some cases in which this strategy can be effective. Avoidance can be used in cases where whatever conflict exists isn't really important to anyone involved and doesn't impact you or the other party in any major way (has no consequences).

✧ **Accommodation.** Resolving conflict with accommodation usually means you'll try to satisfy the other person's wishes, concerns, and needs—usually with some level of effort on your part. The thing to remember with this strategy is that it should only be used if the consequences (or effort you're putting in) don't infringe on your personal boundaries or requires you to ignore your emotions.

An example of this would be to make a commitment to do something that you don't really want to do, say, go to a concert of an artist you don't like with a friend, but you value their friendship, so you're willing to accommodate their desires so you can still spend time together.

- ✧ **Compromising.** This strategy focuses on finding a way to partially satisfy the needs or concerns of everyone involved. Compromising is usually the best resolution in situations where it's impossible to meet everyone's needs, so each person has to be willing and able to compromise on or forfeit certain things.

  For example, you're working on a project with a classmate, the due date is in two days and you're not going to be done in time. You want to ask for an extension but your classmate wants to pull an all-nighter and get it done in time. A potential compromise here could be to meet up after school for the next two days to work on the project more than you were planning to and then decide if it's necessary to ask for more time.

- ✧ **Competing.** This is the opposite of accommodation. Someone who uses this strategy will do everything they can to satisfy their own needs and desires without considering the needs and feelings of those around them—it's usually done at the other party's expense.

  A clear-cut example of this is when you get mad at your friend and give them the silent treatment for not doing what you want to do.

- ✧ **Collaboration.** Collaboration includes finding a way to fully meet the needs of everyone involved (similar to compromising, only it's a win-win situation for all involved instead of needing to give up in some aspects).

An example of this would be if you want to go see a movie and your friend wants to go ice skating, instead of choosing one, you do both (either on the same day or not, either way, everyone gets what they want in the end).

There are many ways to quickly re-regulate your emotional state, such as breathing and grounding exercises. Emotional awareness can be improved by working on your emotional intelligence, which allows you to accept your emotions in real time instead of ignoring or suppressing them. It also allows you to understand yourself, your needs and emotions, as well as those of others, so you're in a better position to negotiate or mediate a resolution.

### *Emotional Intelligence*

Emotional intelligence is one's ability to understand, use, and control your mental state in order to relieve stress, understand where others are coming from (even if they might be going about it in the wrong way), and empathize with them, as well as communicate effectively to avoid misunderstandings.

It's an important aspect of building strong and healthy relationships, achieving personal and professional goals, and making constructive choices with regard to what's most important to you.

You can improve your emotional intelligence by working on self-management, self-awareness, social awareness, and relationship management.

Emotions are like little blocks of information that help us understand ourselves better. But at times, it can also overwhelm us and make us lose control over ourselves. There's a fine line between managing your emotions and suppressing them. Managing your emotions (or self-management) involves accepting and processing them without letting your actions be controlled by them; suppressing your emotions means avoiding them altogether.

Take a moment to think of the relationship you have with your emotions, and this will give you an indication of how well you handle them. Ask yourself the following questions:

✦ Do your emotions flow?

✦ Do you pay attention to your emotions?

✦ Do you sometimes feel your emotions physically in your body?

✦ Do you experience individual emotions, and can you name them effectively?

If your answer to any of these questions is "no," it most likely means that you're not aware of or in touch with your emotions. There are many potential reasons for avoiding strong feelings, such as past trauma, extreme negative experiences with emotions, and the inability to self-regulate.

## Dealing With Disrespect

As mentioned in the previous chapter, your peers or even authority figures (such as your teachers, guardians, elders, or even your parents) might treat you disrespectfully at times. Which is quite honestly ridiculous since they're the ones who should be modeling what it looks like to treat others with kindness and respect. Some people are truly so delusional that they believe they deserve respect without having to respect others in return.

But what exactly is disrespectful behavior? What does it look like? How do you know if someone is being disrespectful?

Disrespect can come in many forms. Disruptive behavior such as angry outbursts, threats, throwing objects, swearing at someone, or even physically hurting someone. Demeaning behavior such as shaming or humiliation, degrading comments, censorship, insults or inappropriate jokes, condescension, or faultfinding (nitpicking everything one does). Intimidation tactics like abuse of power, controlling behavior, arrogance, intentionally ignoring or overstepping boundaries, or bullying. Passive aggression or any insidious behavior such as staring, pointing, rude gestures, lying, belittling, taunting, or exclusion.

The circumstances don't matter. No one has the right to disrespect others, no matter how bad of a mood they're in. One could argue that sometimes disrespect is justified. Being disrespectful to someone who was disrespectful first can feel righteous, moral even. But where does it end? All you're doing is creating a perpetual cycle where you feel justified in disrespecting them back, and then they feel justified in continuing to disrespect you.

By refusing to participate in this snowball effect, you give the perpetrator a chance to think about their actions. Retaliated disrespect is expected. So at the end of the day, everyone focuses on defending their actions instead of reflecting on them and becoming a better person. Granted, some people are so stuck in their ways that no amount of self-reflection will help them be a better person. Don't let that be you.

Here's what you can do when dealing with disrespect from others instead of feeding into their narrow-minded delusions of grandeur:

✧ **Give them the benefit of the doubt.** Disrespect has to be intentional to count as such. So, it's possible that someone's actions might seem disrespectful when it's not actually meant that way. Some forms of disrespect are way less obvious than others. For instance, if someone yells at you, that's obvious and intentional disrespect, but someone not waving back at you when you could've sworn they saw you is less obvious.

It might be possible that they did see you and chose to ignore you; however, if you're friends and have no reason to believe that they don't want to talk to you, chances are they just didn't see you (even if it looked like they did). Giving someone the benefit of the doubt might sometimes mean you let it fly without much thought until it happens again and only then start to investigate or deduce whether they are being disrespectful or just ignorant. If it does continue to happen, or you start to recognize other ways in which they're being disrespectful, you should bring it up and have a discussion about it.

✧ **Call them out.** Another thing someone who is actively and intentionally disrespecting you is not going to expect is someone calling them out on it. "What do you mean by that?" is a simple, non-confrontational question that's pretty effective.

The beauty about this is that it's so low profile; if someone makes a rude remark about you or even about someone else, ask, "What do you mean by that?" This almost forces them to admit that they're being a walking red flag. Ask the question in a way that makes it seem that you're really curious as to what they are trying to say, don't come across as accusatory. You can ask them to elaborate by repeating the question or saying you don't understand, especially when someone is making a joke at your expense.

But it also works to clear up misunderstandings; if they didn't mean something in a bad or disrespectful way, they'd have no issue explaining themselves. And watching them stumble over their words when they realize that they are, in fact, being a soggy pop tart is just an added bonus. It's really a win-win situation; either they clarify what they meant and you realize they were not actually trying to be disrespectful, or they're forced to tell on themselves.

Other ways you can directly call out someone for being openly disrespectful is by saying, "That's a rude thing to say," "Why did you feel the need to say that?" or "That's not that funny though, is it?"

✧ **Try not to take it personally.** Impoliteness of disrespect is more common than you may realize, especially coming from strangers. Someone who's known for their bad attitude isn't going to change their stripes just for you, and a random person pushing past you without so much as an "excuse me" isn't a personal attack on you. So try not to put too much weight behind their rotten personality. Don't let someone who's insignificant to your existence ruin your day or take up mental energy that could be spent doing something more productive.

This will also prevent you from taking your bad mood out on others who don't deserve it. It makes sense; when someone is rude or disrespectful to you, it might disrupt your mood for the whole day leading to you being unfriendly or even rude to others. It might help to think of strangers' disrespect as an isolated incident. Don't let an event that lasted a couple of minutes throw you off for hours.

Now, when it's someone you do know or that you *have* to deal with every day, like a parent, guardian, teacher, or teammate, and you can't avoid interacting with them, and their behavior is causing you distress, that's when you take matters into your own hands by looking at everything else on this list—and decide on a plan of action.

✧ **Remain calm.** This is where many people fail, myself included, sometimes. It's a perfectly reasonable response to lose your cool when someone is continually disrespecting you. But sometimes that's exactly what they want. They want to get a rise out of you. However, this doesn't mean you should just roll over and take it, either.

Staying calm when someone is being disrespectful accomplishes a few things. It shows them that they're not in control of your behavior and that they can't phase you. Even if this is the furthest thing from the truth, even if you're on the verge of throwing hands, try to stay composed. Yes, this is easier said than done, and you might even have to excuse yourself to calm down elsewhere, but the disappointment they will feel afterward when they realize that they were the immature one is worth its weight in gold!

When you do respond or engage (because you have a right to defend and stand up for yourself), don't raise your voice or resort to insulting them. Simply act with tact. Respond with clarifying questions or the classic "What do you mean by that?" Repeat their words back to them and ask them if you understand correctly. Tell them how or why you disagree with what they're saying.

And if you need to, remove yourself from the situation and take some deep, calming breaths—or punch a pillow. Whatever you need to do to let out the frustration (in a healthy, controlled, non-vandalizing way) so they don't get the satisfaction of knowing they'd upset you.

✧ **Vocalize boundaries, and follow through with consequences.** There are certain behaviors that are simply not acceptable. What you deem as unacceptable will vary, but someone screaming and cursing at you is one fairly universal boundary, I feel. So we'll use this as an example.

When someone oversteps a boundary of yours, in this case by yelling or cursing at you, you are well within your right to demand—not ask—them to stop, regardless of who they are. "If you don't stop yelling at me, I'm going to remove myself from this situation," or some variation of this. And if they do continue, be prepared to follow through with the consequences.

✧ **The power of intentionally misunderstanding.** This kind of ties in with asking them to clarify what they meant by whatever they said. When someone is being sarcastic, passive-aggressive, or gives you a backhanded compliment, take it at face value. Thank them or agree with them and move on. If they correct you by saying it wasn't a compliment or that they meant something else, they look like a bad person, and you can then call them out for it. If they ignore it, they are less likely to engage in that behavior around you.

✧ **Snip snip.** In some cases, it won't be possible to cut contact with someone who's constantly disrespectful toward you, but minimizing your interactions (or cutting them off completely) where possible will save you so much mental energy. And staying around people who are disrespectful is never worth it, no matter how cool you think they are.

One thing I've learned in life is that if people tell—or show—you who they are, listen up. It's not exactly a big jump in moral ethics for someone to talk badly about someone else to you and then talk badly about you to whoever is willing to listen. Rudeness is contagious, and it's up to you to decide if it's worth getting infected.

Surround yourself with people who are respectful, and your chances of being disrespected decrease exponentially.

I want to reiterate that it's not possible to avoid being disrespected, especially from people who believe they're superior and deserve respect, simply because they're an adult and you're still a child. And even as an adult, you'll still encounter disrespect from time to time, so getting comfortable with calling it out in a mature way (and even acknowledging and apologizing when you might be the disrespectful one) is an essential life skill.

## Daily Task

Emotional intelligence is an important element in fostering strong connections with people, but it's also necessary for conflict resolution and expressing your emotions, needs, and boundaries in a respectful way—and also respecting the emotions, needs, and boundaries of others.

It allows you to stay calm in times of high stress, take responsibility for your own actions, express your emotions rather than simply unloading them, make others feel heard, and genuinely care about other people and the impact you have on them.

Practicing self-awareness will automatically improve your emotional intelligence, but here's another approach to take on a more proactive role in it:

- ✧ **Allow yourself to be bored.** Get rid of all the distractions for a bit, even if it's just ten minutes a day. Sit with yourself in the present moment without having something to do. It's a scary thought, but it will allow you to connect with and understand your thoughts and feelings better. Just be part of life for a short while every day, no screens, no music, no internet, no games, no hobbies, just you and your brain.

- ✧ **Pay more attention to your emotions.** When simply going about your day, pay attention to how your emotional state changes, and embrace and acknowledge the emotional rollercoaster. It might be unsettling to discover that you feel more sad, angry, or anxious during everyday life than you may have realized—and it can be shameful to admit that sometimes we're not very nice to the people we care about because of it. But it's only through admitting our anger when mom asks us to unload the dishwasher, our anxiety when walking past a group of our peers, or our sadness when thinking of an ex who broke our heart that we understand what makes us tick. And react accordingly.

✧ **React accordingly.** Here's a hard truth to swallow: we can't control our emotions; we can only control how we react to them. So what many people really mean when they say you should learn how to control your emotions is that you should learn how to control your reactions to your emotions.

✧ Recognize what you're feeling and decide if the emotion is warranted or appropriate for the situation, and then react to that emotion accordingly. This doesn't mean the feeling is going to go away. It simply means you're not hurting yourself or others because of it.

✧ **Redirection.** It's easy to look for scapegoats when trying to pinpoint the reason for our emotions. No one wants to be blamed for something, especially when it doesn't feel like it's our fault, but your emotions—regardless of who or what caused them—are your responsibility to deal with. Yes, they're acting like an a-hole, but you can choose to walk away and redirect your emotions elsewhere (in a healthy, non-harmful way).

Your task for today is going to be meditating. Don't worry; it sounds more intimidating than it actually is. You can choose to set a timer for at least five minutes (with a soft and gentle ring to let you know when you're done) or just meditate for as long as you need to. You're simply going to be in the present moment and do a body and mind check-in following a few simple steps:

**Step 1: Get comfortable.** Either sitting or lying down, settle into a position where your body can relax and be comfortable for the next few minutes. It may help if it's somewhere where you feel at ease and won't be disturbed until you're done.

**Step 2: Focus on something.** You can keep your eyes open (but your gaze softened, not focused on any particular object in front of you) or shut. A common thing many people who meditate choose to focus on is their breathing, but you can also focus on a sound or smell.

**Step 3: Stay in the present.** Your mind may drift away; it's normal. Don't get frustrated; simply redirect your attention back to whatever it is you are focusing on (your breathing, a taste, a smell, etc.).

**Step 4: Feel.** Pay attention to any sensations that may be happening in your body and acknowledge them. Feel the way your clothes are touching your skin, feel the couch you're sitting on (or the bed under you). Maybe a soft breeze makes its way through the window and causes your hair to tickle the back of your neck or your face. Maybe you're a bit hungry or thirsty. Maybe your hands are cold. Accept any emotional reaction that might be making its presence known, lean into it and feel your body react to it, allow it to happen. Invite it all in and then submit to it.

**Step 5: Return.** Start by bringing your attention back to your breath, and slowly open your eyes. Move your fingers and toes, then your arms and legs. Do a light stretch if it feels good. You can choose to say a few affirmations or journal your experience. Or just move on with your day from here.

Emotions are neutral, and there's no such thing as good or bad emotions. Yes, anger doesn't feel good, while happiness does, but that doesn't mean anger is inherently bad or that joy is inherently good. They all need to be experienced, processed, and accepted.

CHAPTER 7

# Day 7    SOCIAL SUSTAINABILITY

*Confidence doesn't come out of nowhere. It's a result of something... hours and days and weeks and years of constant work and dedication.*

–Roger Staubach

It's a lot to take in—everything we've discussed so far. I want to remind you that building your social skills, working on self-awareness, establishing connections, and improving your self-esteem is going to take time. Much longer than seven days. However, this book is meant to guide you so you can isolate each of these things and work on them separately.

And while some of them do complement each other or interlace at certain points, if you stick with the program, you will create momentum and stay on track for making progress. Because that's the true goal: progress, no matter how slow.

## Maintaining Momentum

If you've been following along and doing all the daily tasks since day one, you might've already gotten into a slightly different routine than usual. You might still be journaling every day, saying your affirmations, working on improving your social skills in certain areas, stepping out of your comfort zone, making micro-commitments, and having done your first ten-minute "no distractions" exercise.

You're doing the most here. Sticking to a routine that incorporates all of this to some degree—as well as taking care of your physical and mental well-being—is key to sustaining your progress in the long term.

Basically, you need to make habits out of it. I'm sure you know what a habit is; it's a set of actions that—the more you do them—the more ingrained they get and eventually become automatic. Meaning you don't even pay attention to doing them anymore; you just kind of do them without much thought.

There is a three-system loop that's responsible for creating a habit: the cue, the action, and the reward. Once your brain has made a strong connection between the cue and the reward, the action becomes automatic. And while it's hard to form a habit, it's even harder to break out of one (or rather replace it, since established habits don't ever really go away, they get replaced).

So yes, if you're in the habit of avoiding uncomfortable social situations, it's going to take some work to replace that habit with one that's completely new and scary to you. But it's necessary if you want to improve your social skills and connect with people.

## The Routine

A good routine is one that incorporates activities that maintain self-care and promotes personal growth on a daily basis. Remember, the actions you take don't have to be big for results to occur. And whatever your current routine is (even if you don't think you have one), you should never try to change everything all at once because you will lose motivation and fall behind. This will leave you feeling defeated, which will further demotivate you, leading to you giving up on the whole thing entirely.

### *Self-Care*

There's a lot of debate as to what self-care means. But, if you take it at face value, it means taking care of yourself, as the word itself implies. It's things you do to ensure your future self is well—which includes your mind, body, and spirit.

You take care of your body by leading a healthy lifestyle, eating a balanced diet, getting regular exercise, getting enough sleep, getting annual checkups with a doctor, and having healthy hygiene practices (like taking a shower semi-regularly, brushing your teeth daily, etc.).

You take care of your mind by doing things that bring you joy and get rid of stress and mind clutter, such as journaling, art, music, and other hobbies or activities. This can also include things like spending time with friends, being supported and surrounded by people who mean a lot to you, and even playing video games or watching a movie.

You take care of your spirit by doing things that make you feel like you're a part of something greater, something that makes you feel like you have a purpose. This could be helping others in need, volunteering, practicing mindfulness, connecting with nature, or praying to whichever higher power you believe in.

Self-care can also include things that you might not enjoy doing in the moment, but it makes you feel good about yourself afterward. Exercise is a great example of this. You don't enjoy sweating and being out of breath, but you feel a sense of accomplishment and fulfillment knowing every time you do it, you get just a little closer to your fitness goals.

## Personal Growth

This includes things you wish to improve about yourself, whether it's your self-esteem, your social skills, your emotional intelligence, or all of the above. You need to implement and practice it as much as you can—preferably on a daily basis as part of your self-care routine where possible.

Life can get pretty crazy; everything happens so quickly in the era of the internet that our minds sometimes have trouble keeping up. Personal growth can mean a lot of things; it's up to you to decide what your goals are and how you're going to achieve them.

## Goal Setting and Tracking for Personal Growth

Your self-discovery and self-improvement journey will look different depending on what exactly you would like to achieve. There's no communal list where everyone progresses at the same rate or even starts at the same level, which is why it's important to define your goals early on so you can work out a plan of action for achieving them.

Making progress is what gives you the motivation and encouragement to continue, and since self-improvement is very subjective and happens so gradually, you'll need a way to track your progress.

Think of it like this: You need to demolish a house; that's your goal. But not just any house, a brick house. It's a humongous task, so you focus on one thing at a time. You were only given a hammer, so you start chipping away at the mortar, and inch by inch, the bricks underneath get exposed. It feels like you're getting nowhere. Only after an entire day's work do you step back and see that you managed to complete an entire room. After a month, all the mortar on the walls of the entire house is gone, just by you repeating the same action day after day, by being consistent.

The house is still standing, and you still have a long way to go before you achieve your goal, but the work you have done so far was both necessary and meaningful. You might even stumble upon another tool that can get the job done quicker, or at the very least easier, but that doesn't minimize your previous efforts. Similarly, there might be days where all you have is a toothpick and can't get anything done, but again, that doesn't take away the progress you've already made so far.

But determining progress on something that can't physically be observed or quantified is a bit different than simply stepping back and having a looksie. And relying on your subjective memory or intuition to confirm or deny whether you're objectively moving forward or improving is not reliable.

### Goal Setting

Look, the SMART method is a good guide for setting goals: Your goals *should* be specific, measurable, achievable, realistic, and time-bound. And if you want to use the SMART system, be my guest. I'm just personally very bored of it. It's everywhere!

This is why I want to introduce you to a slightly different approach. Starting with determining what your ultimate self-improvement goals are. Think of three of the most prominent challenges in your life right now (that you have control over) and write them down, for example:

✧ I don't have friends.

✧ I don't take care of myself.

✧ My GPA is 2.0.

There might be more, but we're going to focus on three of the challenges that affect you the most first. You're going to look at each of these and conjure up a unique goal based on what you want the end result to look like. Based on the above-mentioned examples, let's go with the following:

✧ Become part of a friend group.

✧ Get into a consistent self-care routine.

✧ Raise my GPA to 3.0 (so I can at least get into college).

This is your metaphorical brick house. You're going to craft a plan of action for the most important one and make a start. In my opinion, a self-care routine is the most important goal to achieve out of all three on the list. Because when you're taking care of yourself, you feel better, and when you feel better, you'll have the mental and physical capacity to tackle the rest of your problems.

I'm going to start by evaluating my current self-care routine: Doom scrolling social media until two a.m. in the morning, yes. Haven't had a glass of pure water in six months, check. Forgets to brush teeth—oh, don't you dare judge me! This is a safe space, remember?

So, it's not… ideal, but we know what we're working with now; we have a starting point. I would do some research and figure out what a healthy self-care routine generally looks like. Getting enough sleep, eating a balanced diet, drinking enough water, keeping up with personal hygiene, and moving your body are the bare basics of self-care. Simple enough.

What I'm *not* going to do is completely up-root my daily life and overwhelm myself by trying to change every single unhealthy habit at once until I inevitably give up and go back to square one. Instead, I'm going to isolate one factor, in this case, increasing my water intake.

My initial goal is to drink a single glass of water every day for at least a week. I'll set a reminder if I have to, or combine it with another task so I don't forget (like drinking a glass of water right after I take a hot shower since that is when I usually feel thirsty—and I would ignore it). I would reward myself every day that I manage to drink a glass of water and be kind to myself if I do happen to miss a day here and there.

After I have taken to the habit of drinking a full glass of water every day, I would move on to the next milestone: Drinking two glasses of water a day. Once that habit has been established, I have significantly increased my water intake from what it was—which was zero. By this point, I'd be pretty chuffed with myself, call it a win, and move on to a different factor of building a healthier self-care routine.

Your goal is your desired result; your milestones are how you get there. Jumping from drinking no water a day to the recommended amount, which is eight, is unrealistic. And honestly, even if you stick to two glasses of water a day for months before you try to increase it again, it's still an improvement!

You should also only focus on one, maybe two, manageable milestones per goal at a time. For example, drinking one glass of water a day and going to sleep half an hour earlier than I normally would. Only once I've gotten my water intake and sleep to where it needs to be would I move on to the next ones: Diet and movement. Again, small changes and milestones that are sustainable are the way to go.

Instead of only having chocolate as a snack, I'd have chocolate-covered strawberries; instead of only having Cheerios for breakfast, I'd also have some full-cream yogurt alongside it. A healthy, balanced diet is more about adding beneficial foods rather than taking 'unhealthy' stuff away, but I digress. For more movement, I'd add a five-minute walk around the block to my daily routine, obviously while listening to music, an audiobook, or my favorite podcast.

After months of consistent effort, I'd have gotten to a point where my self-care routine was solid. Sure, there might be days where I skip breakfast or don't take a walk, or still forget to brush my teeth, but 80% of the time, I nail it. I'm happy with a B minus, and you should be, too!

Now, whatever goal you choose to start with next will depend on the priority, importance, and effect it has on your life. Let's say I have less than a year before I need to start applying for colleges or universities. And I'm definitely going to need a scholarship. In this case, I would prioritize my goal of raising my GPA over my goal of becoming part of a friend group.

While still maintaining my new self-care routine, I would brainstorm what I could do to raise my grades. Summer school, online classes, and getting a tutor are all feasible options. On top of this, I can revise my textbooks (maybe going over previous chapters and highlighting what I'm struggling with) and ask for extra-credit assignments. I might do weekly study reviews to make sure I understand the work that was covered and make notes as I go so I have summaries of the important stuff when studying for tests. I would put more effort into homework, assignments, and projects and ask for help if I needed it.

There are plenty of YouTube channels dedicated to breaking down the high school curriculum content for any class so it's easier to memorize and understand. I would take full advantage of this resource, too. But I would also schedule rest or off days, days where I do the bare minimum, and make sure I have time for self-care as well as things I enjoy, like hobbies. Burnout takes years to recover from; you don't want that before you even start college or enter the workforce.

Last but certainly not least, I would sprinkle in small steps toward making friends while pursuing my other milestones relating to self-care and raising my grade. For example, my first milestone would be to do some introspection (as discussed in the previous chapters) and figure out who I am, what's important to me, the type of friendships I want, and the type of people who I want to be surrounded with.

Then, I'd observe my peers and identify who I'm most interested in being friends with, the kind ones, the non-judgmental ones (they're rare, but they exist), the ones who have the same interests and values as me, the ones who are applying to the same colleges as I am. This information will help establish an initial connection—albeit a rather superficial one. It will take time and effort to nurture the connection so a friendship can grow from it.

In the meantime, I'd also work on my self-confidence and self-esteem so I'm better able to showcase who I really am and not be so afraid to open up to and trust other people.

## Goal Tracking

We are constantly changing, whether we're actively trying to or not. Our experiences, thoughts, and emotions create our perspective. A simple example of this is to think about something you didn't know when you were younger and how it has changed or shaped your current understanding of the world.

For example, when I was younger, I thought turning the car light on while driving was illegal because, well, my dad told me so. As an adult, I know that it's not actually illegal; it just drains the battery. My dad told me it was illegal because I wouldn't have been able to understand the consequences otherwise. He was just trying to avoid being stranded on the side of the highway with a dead battery.

We don't keep track of these little changes and bits of information we learn or figure out on our own. Until one day, you take a general knowledge quiz at 12 a.m. out of boredom and you realize that you didn't even know a lot of the things you know or remember where you learned them from. Personal growth is just like that, you hoard and implement little changes and habits until you're a completely different person, and yet, you didn't even notice it while it was happening.

How do you keep track of a concept such as self-improvement? How do you measure whether your self-confidence has leveled up? It's not like you have a stats menu where you can see your progress on a bar. Maybe Elon Musk can add that as a feature or app for his brain chip once it passes human trials.

Tracking your personal growth is as simple as finding a way to document it. Journaling can be a good way to do this, but while it can give you an overall idea of how your inner monologue and perspective have changed, it's not very specific.

You'll need to look at your goals and determine what the best way to track them would be—using my three goals from before, I'd say that for my self-care goal, a daily habit tracker is a good idea. For improving my grades, a spreadsheet that documents my progress in a line graph is straightforward and sufficient. And for building and tracking personal relationships, I'd add it to my daily habit tracker and put a symbol or draw a little smiley face every time I initiate a conversation with someone.

With regard to a timeline, I'd be lenient with it and not be too hard on myself if I don't complete milestones within the given timeframe. You really can't put a time limit on personal growth since you can't possibly know how long it's going to take. In most cases, with regard to personal growth, a due date is more so to keep yourself accountable. The only thing on my list that will need a set timeframe is raising my GPA before college applications open.

Your emotional health or mood can be tracked through a week/month/year in pixels: That's where you give all your feelings a color key and color in one square per day based on your most prominent mood for the day (red is anger, yellow is happy, blue is anxious, and so on). Your skills can be tracked by means of having a sketchbook for tracking art skills, recording yourself practicing, or anything else that allows you to physically see your improvement over time.

Another, more "out there" way to track your progress is by putting yourself to the test and seeing whether you would fare better now than you would've previously. This is for things like social skills, where there really is no other way to track your progress and new knowledge other than to just go out and try it out.

And obviously, you'll record your milestones and goals so you can celebrate once you've reached them!

## *Motivation*

Your goals, milestones, and the approach you take to achieve them will look completely different to everyone. But any goal has to be important to you because if it isn't, you don't have any reason or motivation to complete it or make progress with it. So go ahead and ask yourself why, "Why is this goal important to me?"

Using my three example goals of being part of a friend circle, improving my self-care, and raising my GPA, the reasons are pretty self-explanatory. Having friends who support me is important for my mental health and it would make me feel less lonely. Self-care is equivalent to self-love, which will raise my self-image and ensure I stay healthy. Raising my GPA means I get into the college of my choice, which will allow me to pursue my dream job.

However, even when your goals are important to you, it doesn't mean your motivation will last. Motivation is just excitement rebranded. And since excitement is just an emotion, it's not enough to keep you going in the long term. I'm telling you now that you will inevitably lose motivation, probably quicker than you realize. Whether it's because you forget your motive behind them or get bored or distracted, it's how the cookie crumbles.

This is why you shouldn't rely on motivation to fuel you. Don't get me wrong, motivation is a great thing to have, but it shouldn't be the driving force behind your actions. If you wait for motivation to show up in order to take action, you will go long periods of time without making any effort toward progress at all.

It might help to think of motivation as the effect and not the cause, meaning that motivation isn't necessary for action but rather the result of action. And sure, in some cases, you might see something online or even in real life that inspires or motivates you, but I would say that's the lowest form of motivation that exists.

No, what's truly motivating is seeing the fruits of your labor—sticking to the plan even though you don't feel inspired or motivated to do so. The feeling you get when you realize you have been severely underestimating yourself all this time. Motivation *is* the reward. It's a release of dopamine—the feel-good hormone.

So, what *should* you then rely on to stay consistent?

Commitment.

Yes, it's hard. Losing sight of a goal, taking longer to reach a milestone than you anticipated, and backtracking by skipping multiple days are all things that will make you feel bad about yourself and just revert back to your old ways, giving up on the whole idea of self-improvement. It all comes down to commitment.

The journey to self-improvement is not linear. And what many people fail to understand is that commitment doesn't guarantee success. It means staying committed to a goal even when you regress or fail altogether. It means trying again no matter what others might say or think, or even what you might say or think of yourself.

Have the commitment of a toddler. It takes roughly two years before a child starts walking confidently, without support, and without falling down every two minutes. At no point has any physically-abled toddler decided that walking isn't for them because they have stumbled one too many times. It takes even longer for them to start talking fluently, but they don't give up. Why? Because they don't judge themselves—mainly because they don't yet have the mental capability to do so yet, but that's beside the point.

What would happen if you let go of the shame, guilt, or judgment that comes with perceived failure? What would happen if you completely redefine what failure and success mean to you?

Is failure the act of not meeting your own or others' expectations, or is it the lack of taking action in the first place? Does failure determine your value and worth, or does it simply mean that you need a different approach? Is failure a destination? And if it is, wouldn't that mean that you can only fail when you stop trying?

Failure can't be measured. Not in a way that's substantial or objective, anyway. It's purely based on opinions and imaginative social constructs. Your own included! Change the way you determine and view failure because nothing destroys commitment quite like the belief that you have already failed.

## Daily Task

Your daily task for today is going to be about your daily routine and what small changes you can make so you can achieve your goals. You're going to start by mapping out your current routine. Think about what you do on most days from the moment you wake up to when you get back in bed, don't worry about time stamps; just keep it as detailed and accurate as you can.

Can you identify anything you're doing (or not doing) that's holding you back from achieving your goals? Maybe you try your best to fly under the radar at school, have no hobbies or extracurriculars, the only two places you go are to school and back home (even on weekends), and you spend more hours on your phone than the amount of sleep you get per night.

Now you're going to find one small thing you can do differently that will result in a slightly better outcome in the future. For example, sacrifice ten minutes of your screen time every day to do something that either includes self-care or self-improvement, like sitting in the sun, going for a short walk, or self-reflection. Or having a breakfast meal that consists of something other than a single cup of coffee. Or blocking out time to spend with people in your life who you value and care about.

You'll continue to accumulate all these little habits one at a time that make you feel better about yourself, and eventually, you'll be resilient enough, confident enough, and strong enough to face and recover from all the discomfort and curveballs that life throws at you—because sometimes life is simply unavoidable.

# CONCLUSION

One thing that you learn quite quickly as you grow up is that no one—regardless of your social or economic status—makes it through life without getting a few scars along the way. In the hypothetical war zone that is life, some may lose limbs while others only end up with bruises, but getting hurt to some extent is inevitable.

We can't control our emotions, but we can learn to control what we do about them and how we express them. And how you react to your emotions will change your perception of the world in the long run by rewiring your brain. This is why every journal entry, every thought you challenge, every positive affirmation, and every milestone you achieve counts. Every effort and any amount of progress is worth celebrating.

Low self-esteem (and, as a result, low confidence and social anxiety) has many roots and can take on many forms. But I can tell you this: It's never your fault. Having unsupportive parents with unrealistic goals, narcissistic friends, having gone or are going through a stressful period, exhibiting signs of a mental health disorder, or doing poorly in school are all circumstances that are not in your control—and they create the perfect breeding ground for self-doubt and resentment.

Maybe you avoid conflict because it never ends well and leaves you triggered and emotional for days. It never feels like you're wanted or included, so it's easier and less painful to simply remove yourself from the discussion before others make the decision for you. You're so scared of failing and what the consequences would be that you can never take accountability for your mistakes or learn anything from them—because the fear of punishment overpowers the lesson behind it. You never seem to do anything right, so you avoid doing it at all, or you lack the motivation to even try because every time you do, you hear that little voice in your head telling you you're not good enough, not smart enough, not funny enough, not talented enough.

You look at what others your age have been able to accomplish and you feel angry, jealous, or spiteful. You're being compared to others by the people who are supposed to love and encourage you. How can you be happy for them if their success is being used against you? How can you be friends with them if they're a constant reminder of your incompetence?

It doesn't always take extreme circumstances to affect your self-image. And while a lot of it comes down to how you were raised, that's not always the case. The seed of doubt can be planted by a random comment from a teacher, a disappointed sigh from your father, or a bad grade on a test you actually studied for. If enough of these seeds are sowed, eventually, one will break through the soil. From then on, you'll look for any and all justifications as to why you keep on watering it:

"Why would they want to talk to me?"

"It's not even worth trying."

"I'm the only person I can trust."

It happens so gradually that you don't even realize it until one day, someone asks you why you're always so quiet and withdrawn, why you never come out of your room, or why you choose to be alone. It's because the world is a scary place for an impressionable young mind. It's because your assumptions and past experiences keep you hidden and scared to show the world who you really are. As a result, no one will know who you really are—not even you.

This unstable sense of self will follow you around until you've addressed it. You're at the age now where you're expected to know what your ultimate goals and dreams are in life. Only, you've been so focused on what you're *not* that you forgot to pay attention to what you *are*.

Here's the thing, though, when your brain has convinced you that no one likes you, you avoid others to avoid the emotional turmoil. When you don't practice social skills, they don't develop or strengthen.

So, you don't see yourself as worthy; you assume others think the same, and you don't know what to say or how to react in certain social situations. You're afraid you're going to embarrass yourself, and you're overthinking others' reactions, doubting their intentions, and going above and beyond to avoid spending time out in public. You might even break out in a sweat, experience heart palpitations, or have full-blown panic attacks during social events, or even while talking to someone you know well.

It's hard to connect with someone when it feels like you're fighting for your life. But by taking small steps at a time, using my version of the seven-day system, you can overcome your insecurities and build your confidence until nothing anyone does or says can shake the ground beneath your feet.

And as much as none of this is your fault, it's your life we're talking about here and, ultimately, your responsibility to take the reins. But do me a favor and try to smell the flowers along the way because as much as life can suck sometimes, there will be moments when everything is worth it. Savor those moments when they come.

You might be thinking that you have such a long way to go still, and you're right. But don't focus on the end goal because when it comes to self-improvement, there really isn't one. Don't look too far into the future either; just focus on your next step, and once you've taken it, the next one after that.

You don't have to be the best; you just have to be slightly better than you were last week.

# THANK YOU

Thank you so much for purchasing my book.

The marketplace is filled with dozens and dozens of other similar books but you took a chance and chose this one. And I hope it was well worth it.

So again, THANK YOU for getting this book and for making it all the way to the end.

Before you go, I wanted to ask you for one small favor.

**Could you please consider posting a review for my book on the platform? Posting a review is the best and easiest way to support the work of independent authors like me.**

Your feedback will help me to keep writing the kind of books that will help you get the results you want. It would mean a lot to me to hear from you.

Leave a Review on Amazon US →

Leave a Review on Amazon UK→

# ABOUT THE AUTHOR

Emily Carter is an author who loves helping teens with their biggest turning point in life, adulting. She grew up in New York and is happily married to her high school sweetheart. She also has two of her own children.

In her free time, Emily is an avid volunteer at a local food bank and enjoys hiking, traveling, and reading books on personal development. With over a decade of experience in the education and parenting field she has seen the difference that good parenting and the right tips can make in a teenager's life. She is now an aspiring writer through which she shares her insights and advice on raising happy, healthy, and resilient children, teens, and young adults.

Emily's own struggles with navigating adulthood and overcoming obstacles inspired her to write. She noticed a gap in education regarding teaching essential life skills to teens and young adults. She decided to write comprehensive guides covering everything from money and time management to job searching and communication skills. Emily hopes her book will empower teens and young adults to live their best lives and reach their full potential.

To find more of her books, visit her Amazon Author page at:

https://www.amazon.com/author/emily-carter

# REFERENCES

A Little Dose Of Happy. (2022, August 15). *9 Tips for cultivating relationships that last - a little dose of happy*. Aldohappy. https://aldohappy.com/cultivating-relationships

Abrahamsen, S. (2019, August 28). *5 Easy ways to track your personal growth*. Little Coffee Fox. https://littlecoffeefox.com/track-your-personal-growth/

Allen, R. (2011, April 1). *How to challenge your beliefs*. https://www.rogerkallen.com/how-to-challenge-your-beliefs/

Angel, D. (2016, December 28). *The four types of conversations: Debate, dialogue, discourse, and diatribe*. https://davidwangel.com/the-opportune-conflict/2016/12/28/the-four-types-of-conversations-debate-dialogue-discourse-and-diatribe

AZ Quotes. (n.d.). *Top 25 first impression quotes (of 109)*. Retrieved July 4, 2023, from https://www.azquotes.com/quotes/topics/first-impression.html#:~:text=You%20never%20get%20a%20second%20chance%20to%20make%20a%20first%20impression.&text=You%20only%20have%20one%20first

Baller, E. (2016, May 27). *10 Ways to cultivate a positive mindset and change your life*. Tiny Buddha. https://tinybuddha.com/blog/10-ways-cultivate-positive-mindset-change-life/

Barclays Life Skills. (n.d.). *What are your strengths? - 5 ways to find out.* https://barclayslifeskills.com/i-want-to-choose-my-next-step/school/5-ways-to-find-out-what-you-re-good-at/

Barrier, J. (n.d.). *8 Strategies for meaningful conversations - improve your skills.* Preach It, Teach It. Retrieved July 6, 2023, from https://preachitteachit.org/articles/detail/eight-simple-strategies-to-have-meaningful-conversations/

Baulch, J. (2016, September 5). *Thought challenging when negative.* Inner Melbourne Psychology. https://www.innermelbpsychology.com.au/thought-challenging/#:~:text=Break%20your%20thoughts%20down%20into

Carnahan, L. (2022, June 2). *How to hold a conversation and build deeper connections.* Vector Marketing. https://www.thevectorimpact.com/how-to-hold-a-conversation/

Cherry, K. (2017). *Understanding body language and facial expressions.* Verywell Mind. https://www.verywellmind.com/understand-body-language-and-facial-expressions-4147228

Cherry, K. (2022, November 8). *How our brain neurons can change over time from life's experience.* Verywell Mind. https://www.verywellmind.com/what-is-brain-plasticity-2794886

Cherry, K. (2023a, February 22). *What are the 9 types of nonverbal communication?* Verywell Mind. https://www.verywellmind.com/types-of-nonverbal-communication-2795397#:~:text=Nonverbal%20communication%20means%20conveying%20information

Cherry, K. (2023b, March 10). *What is self-awareness?* Verywell Mind. https://www.verywellmind.com/what-is-self-awareness-2795023

## References

Cuncic, A. (2019). *Things to start doing if you have social anxiety disorder.* Verywell Mind. https://www.verywellmind.com/social-anxiety-disorder-tips-3024209

Cuncic, A. (2023, February 15). *10 Best and worst small talk topics.* Verywell Mind. https://www.verywellmind.com/small-talk-topics-3024421

Davenport, B. (2022, July 1). *75 Confidence-boosting positive affirmations for teens.* Live Bold and Bloom. https://liveboldandbloom.com/07/mindfulness/positive-affirmations-teens

Davis, T. (2019, April 11). *15 Ways to build a growth mindset.* Psychology Today. https://www.psychologytoday.com/za/blog/click-here-happiness/201904/15-ways-build-growth-mindset

Drillinger, M. (2020, February 25). *6 Ways to make friends when you have social anxiety.* Healthline. https://www.healthline.com/health/anxiety/how-to-make-friends-when-you-have-social-anxiety#2.-Fight

Eatough, E. (2022, January 12). *25 Toxic personality traits to spot in yourself and others.* Betterup. https://www.betterup.com/blog/toxic-traits

Eisler, M. (2019, April 19). *15 Ways to declutter your mind.* The Chopra Center. https://chopra.com/articles/15-ways-to-declutter-your-mind

Elcomblus. (2020, December 18). *Elements of verbal communication.* https://www.elcomblus.com/elements-of-verbal-communication/

Gordon, J. P. (2019, November 7). *Low self-esteem and social anxiety.* Counselling Directory. https://www.counselling-directory.org.uk/memberarticles/low-self-esteem-and-social-anxiety#:~:text=This%20very%20low%20self%2Desteem

Gupta, S. (2022, September 14). *What is self-acceptance?* Verywell Mind. https://www.verywellmind.com/self-acceptance-characteristics-importance-and-tips-for-improvement-6544468

Hailey, L. (2022, November 9). *15 Effective ways to connect with absolutely anyone, anytime.* Science of People. https://www.scienceofpeople. com/how-to-connect-with-others/#:~:text=A%20struggle%20to%20 connect%20could

Holland, K. (2018). *Positive self-talk: Benefits and techniques.* Healthline. https://www.healthline.com/health/positive-self-talk

Hull, R. H. (2016). *The art of nonverbal communication in practice.* The Hearing Journal, 69(5), 22. https://doi.org/10.1097/01.hj.0000483270.59643.cc

Incledon, N. (2018, April 11). *How low self-esteem affects relationships.* Peacefulmind.com.au. https://peacefulmind.com.au/2018/04/11/ how-low-self-esteem-affects-relationships/#:~:text=Low%20 self%2Desteem%20can%20give

Kentucky Counselling Center. (2021, May 14). *How to build mental resilience.* https://kentuckycounselingcenter.com/how-to-build-mental- resilience/

Kottke, J. (2018, May 17). *The respect of personhood vs the respect of authority.* https://kottke.org/18/05/the-respect-of-personhood- vs-the-respect-of-authority

Kropf, J. (2023, May 15). *50 Easy ways to get out of your comfort zone.* Healthy Happy Impactful. https://healthyhappyimpactful.com/ ways-get-out-comfort-zone-quotes/

Lawler, M. (2022, August 26). *How to start a self-care routine you'll follow.* Everyday Health. https://www.everydayhealth.com/self-care/ start-a-self-care-routine/

Liles, M. (2021, February 21). *101 Uplifting confidence quotes for days you're struggling with low self-esteem.* Parade. https://parade.com/989608/ marynliles/confidence-quotes/

*References*

Lindberg, S. (2020, November 26). *Self-Improvement goal setting tips.* Verywell Mind. https://www.verywellmind.com/tips-for-goal-setting-self-improvement-4688587

Lumen Learning. (n.d.). *Effective communication.* Lumen Learning.com. Retrieved July 7, 2023, from https://courses.lumenlearning.com/suny-monroecc-hed110/chapter/communication/

Manson, M. (2019, April 11). *5 Skills to help you develop emotional intelligence.* https://markmanson.net/emotional-intelligence

Matthews, D. (2020, January 9). *How to identify your limiting beliefs and get over them.* Lifehack. https://www.lifehack.org/858652/limiting-beliefs

Mayo Clinic. (2020, April 22). *A beginner's guide to meditation.* https://www.mayoclinic.org/tests-procedures/meditation/in-depth/meditation/art-20045858#:~:text=%22Meditation%2C%20which%20is%20the%20practice

Melinda. (2019, June 3). Social anxiety disorder. Help Guide. https://www.helpguide.org/articles/anxiety/social-anxiety-disorder.htm

Merabet, L. B., & Pascual-Leone, A. (2009). *Neural reorganization following sensory loss: The opportunity of change.* Nature Reviews Neuroscience, 11(1), 44–52. https://doi.org/10.1038/nrn2758

Merriam-Webster. (n.d.). *Definition of respect.* https://www.merriam-webster.com/dictionary/respect#:~:text=%3A%20high%20or%20special%20regard%20%3A%20esteem

Merriam-Webster. (2020). *Definition of self-confidence.* https://www.merriam-webster.com/dictionary/self-confidence

Mindtools. (n.d.). *Empathy at work.* https://www.mindtools.com/agz0gft/empathy-at-work

Morin, A. (2022, July 28). *5 Ways to start boosting your self-confidence today.* Verywell Mind. https://www.verywellmind.com/how-to-boost-your-self-confidence-4163098

Nemours Kids Health. (n.d.). *5 Ways to (respectfully) disagree (for teens).* Kids Health. https://kidshealth.org/en/teens/tips-disagree.html

Nguyen, S. O. (2023, January 31). *88 Daily journal prompts on life, love, and gratitude.* Parade: Entertainment, Recipes, Health, Life, Holidays. https://parade.com/1308069/steph-nguyen/journaling-prompts/

NHS. (2021, February 1). *Raising low self-esteem.* https://www.nhs.uk/mental-health/self-help/tips-and-support/raise-low-self-esteem/

Nigam, D. (2023, April 13). *Elements of verbal and non verbal communication.* https://www.linkedin.com/pulse/elements-verbal-non-communication-divakar-nigam

Perry, E. (2022, June 7). *20 Personal values examples to help you find your own.* Better Up. https://www.betterup.com/blog/personal-values-examples

Perry, E. (2023, March 14). *How to build confidence: A guide to doing it right.* Better Up. https://www.betterup.com/blog/how-to-build-confidence

Peterson, T. J. (2022, March 25). *What is self-confidence?* Healthy Place. https://www.healthyplace.com/self-help/self-confidence/what-is-self-confidence

Pollack, J. (2021, April 19). *Tip #7: Challenge your beliefs.* Pollack Peace Building. https://pollackpeacebuilding.com/blog/tip-7-challenge-your-beliefs/

Portland Community College. (2020, March 11). *What are the five conflict resolution strategies?* Climb. https://climb.pcc.edu/blog/what-are-the-five-conflict-resolution-strategies#:~:text=Identify%20specific%20points%20of%20disagreement

Price, C. (2018, January 8). *Strengthening your teen's social and conversation abilities.* Hey Sigmund. https://www.heysigmund.com/strengthening-teens-social-conversation-abilities/

Pyramid Psychology. (2021, June 14). *4 Conversation tips for teens: Getting past the shy.* https://pyramidpsychology.com/how-to-get-past-the-shy-4-conversation-tips-for-teens/

Quizzclub. (2017, April 7). *"You never get a second chance to make a first impression" was an ad slogan for which company?* https://quizzclub.com/trivia/you-never-get-a-second-chance-to-make-a-first-impression-was-an-ad-slogan-for-which-company/answer/152271/

Rao, S. T. S., Asha, M. R., Rao, J. K. S., & Vasudevaraju, P. (2009). The biochemistry of belief. *Indian Journal of Psychiatry, 51*(4), 239. https://doi.org/10.4103/0019-5545.58285

Ratey, J. J. (2019, October 24). *Can exercise help treat anxiety?* Harvard Health Blog. https://www.health.harvard.edu/blog/can-exercise-help-treat-anxiety-2019102418096#:~:text=How%20does%20exercise%20help%20ease

Raypole, C. (2019, February 25). *How systematic desensitization can help you overcome fear.* Healthline Media. https://www.healthline.com/health/systematic-desensitization

Raypole, C. (2020, February 27). *Self-Actualization: What it is and how to achieve it.* Healthline. https://www.healthline.com/health/self-actualization

Reach Out. (2019). *Self-esteem and teenagers.* https://parents.au.reachout.com/common-concerns/everyday-issues/self-esteem-and-teenagers

Reynolds, N. (2020, October 12). *10 Important social skills you need to teach your teen now.* Raising Teens Today. https://raisingteenstoday.com/10-important-social-skills-you-need-to-teach-your-teen-now/

Sander, V. (2021, August 18). *How to improve your social skills - the complete guide.* SocialSelf. https://socialself.com/blog/improve-social-skills/

Sander, V. (2023, January 4). *16 Ways to respond when someone is disrespectful to you.* SocialSelf. https://socialself.com/blog/someone-disrespectful/

Schultz, K. (n.d.). *Self-Image: Definition, issues, & tips.* The Berkeley Well-Being Institute. https://www.berkeleywellbeing.com/self-image.html

Segal, J., Robinson, L., & Smith, M. (2019, March 21). *Conflict resolution skills.* Help Guide. https://www.helpguide.org/articles/relationships-communication/conflict-resolution-skills.htm

Segal, J., Smith, M., Robinson, L., & Shubin, J. (2020, October). *Improving emotional intelligence.* Help Guide. https://www.helpguide.org/articles/mental-health/emotional-intelligence-eq.htm#:~:text=Emotional%20intelligence%20(otherwise%20known%20as

Shah, M. (2022, January 8). *Challenges are what make life interesting and overcoming them is what makes life meaningful.* Set Quotes. https://www.setquotes.com/challenges-are-what-make-life-interesting/

Skills You Need. (2011). *What are social skills?* https://www.skillsyouneed.com/ips/social-skills.html

Smith, J. (2020, September 25). *Growth vs fixed mindset: How what you think affects what you achieve.* Mindset Health. https://www.mindsethealth.com/matter/growth-vs-fixed-mindset

Smith, S. (2018, April 10). *5-4-3-2-1 Coping technique for anxiety.* University of Rochester Medical Center. https://www.urmc.rochester.edu/

behavioral-health-partners/bhp-blog/april-2018/5-4-3-2-1-coping-technique-for-anxiety.aspx

Social Skill Center. (2021, February 19). *The difference between verbal and nonverbal communication.* https://socialskillscenter.com/the-difference-between-verbal-and-nonverbal-communication/#:~:text=There%20are%20two%20primary%20forms

Sonder Wellness. (2022, August 22). *Healthy friendships: 6 Key ingredients.* https://www.sonderwellness.com/blog/2022/08/22/healthy-friendships/

Stenvinkel, M. (2016, October 3). *13 Things to do instead of comparing yourself to others.* Tiny Buddha. https://tinybuddha.com/blog/13-things-instead-comparing-others/

Suni, E., & Dimitriu, A. (2020, September 18). *Anxiety and sleep.* Sleep Foundation. https://www.sleepfoundation.org/mental-health/anxiety-and-sleep#:~:text=Sleep%20deprivation%20can%20worsen%20anxiety

This Way Up. (n.d.). *How to deal with social anxiety.* https://thiswayup.org.au/learning-hub/social-anxiety-explained/

University of Texas. (2020, November 3). *How much of communication is nonverbal?* https://online.utpb.edu/about-us/articles/communication/how-much-of-communication-is-nonverbal/#:~:text=It%20was%20Albert%20Mehrabian%2C%20a

Voss, P., Thomas, M. E., Cisneros-Franco, J. M., & de Villers-Sidani, É. (2017). Dynamic brains and the changing rules of neuroplasticity: Implications for learning and recovery. *Frontiers in Psychology, 8*(1657). https://doi.org/10.3389/fpsyg.2017.01657

Wallis, L. J., Virányi, Z., Müller, C. A., Serisier, S., Huber, L., & Range, F. (2016). Aging effects on discrimination learning, logical reasoning and memory in pet dogs. *AGE, 38*(1). https://doi.org/10.1007/s11357-015-9866-x

Warley, S. (n.d.). *How to practice self-awareness.* Life Skills That Matter. https://lifeskillsthatmatter.com/podcast/how-to-practice-self-awareness/

Waters, S. (2021, November 15). *How to carry a conversation — the art of making connections.* Www.betterup.com. https://www.betterup.com/blog/how-to-carry-a-conversation

Westside DBT. (n.d.). *The neuroscience of change—or how to reset your brain.* Retrieved June 28, 2023, from https://westsidedbt.com/the-neuroscience-of-change-or-how-to-reset-your-brain/

Yeager, D. S., Hanselman, P., Walton, G. M., Murray, J. S., Crosnoe, R., Muller, C., Tipton, E., Schneider, B., Hulleman, C. S., Hinojosa, C. P., Paunesku, D., Romero, C., Flint, K., Roberts, A., Trott, J., Iachan, R., Buontempo, J., Yang, S. M., Carvalho, C. M., & Hahn, P. R. (2019). A national experiment reveals where a growth mindset improves achievement. *Nature, 573*(573). https://doi.org/10.1038/s41586-019-1466-